Shaping School Culture

Terrence E. Deal
Kent D. Peterson

Shaping School Culture

The Heart of Leadership

Jossey-Bass Publishers
San Francisco

Jossey-Bass books and products are available through most bookstores. To contact Jossey-Bass directly, call (888) 378–2537, fax to (800) 605–2665, or visit our website at www.josseybass.com.

Substantial discounts on bulk quantities of Jossey-Bass books are available to corporations, professional associations, and other organizations. For details and discount information, contact the special sales department at Jossey-Bass.

TCF Manufactured in the United States of America on Lyons Falls Turin Book. This paper is acid-free and 100 percent totally chlorine-free.

Library of Congress Cataloging-in-Publication Data

Deal, Terrence E.
    Shaping school culture : the heart of leadership / Terrence E. Deal, Kent D. Peterson. — 1st ed.
      p.   cm. — (The Jossey-Bass education series)
    Includes bibliographical references and index.
    ISBN 0-7879-4342-8 (cloth : acid-free paper)
    1. Educational leadership. 2. School environment. 3. Educational change.
4. Educational leadership—Case studies. I. Peterson, Kent D. II. Title. III. Series.
    LB2805.D34   1999
    371.2—ddc21   98-40112

HB Printing   10 9 8 7 6 5 4   FIRST EDITION

The Jossey-Bass Education Series

Contents

Part Two: The Leadership Challenge

Preface

This book represents a major reworking of an idea that started in 1990 as *The Principal's Role in Shaping School Culture*—a best-seller for the U.S. Department of Education. It has been substantially expanded and developed, and now appears as this book: *Shaping School Culture: The Heart of Leadership*. We added significant new material, expanded illustrations, and introduced some new ideas. We received a lot of help in our rewrite from school leaders. From across the country and indeed the world, readers of *The Principal's Role* have shared ideas and examples. They tell us that stories and examples make a difference to them in the way they think about their schools and deal with the cultures in which they work.

It is clearly time to reconsider and rethink the issues and importance of school culture in today's educational environment. There is no doubt in our minds that students have the right to the best schools we can provide. There is also little doubt that teaching staff and administrators can lead the way to successful cultures where all students learn. Of late, far too much emphasis has been given to reforming schools from the outside, through policies and mandates. Too little attention has been paid to how schools can be shaped from within, as our colleague Roland Barth (1991) demonstrates. The research and examples of excellent practice that we draw from show that top-flight schools are possible in every community. This book pulls together the best that we know about culture to provide insights and examples of ways teachers, administrators, parents, and community can create positive, caring, and intellectually challenging schools.

The importance of school culture and the symbolic roles of leaders in shaping cultural patterns and practices remain at the core of this book. While policymakers and reformers are pressing for new structures and more rational assessments, it is important to remember that these changes cannot be successful without cultural support. School cultures, in short, are key to school achievement and student learning. In this book, we have expanded the research base demonstrating how culture influences school functioning.

In our look at the importance of mission and purpose, we added new material because mission and purpose are central features of culture. We added examples of the types of rituals and traditions found in quality schools. We added new case examples of the ways stories and history are used to build commitment and motivation. We added important new illustrations of symbols in architecture as well as in action. We integrated original case studies of culture building and development into relevant chapters; before, they were separate and seemed to be add-ons. We added considerable case material to the ways leaders shape culture, with three new roles and numerous useful examples. We added a significant new chapter on "toxic" cultures—negative places where the rituals, traditions, and values have gone sour and threaten the very soul of a school. We expanded our discussion of the connection between the culture of the school and the culture of the local community. We think this now receives the attention it deserves.

There are new examples and totally new cases collected while we were working with schools across the globe, including schools in British Columbia, London, Singapore, Toronto, and Norway. A number of excellent examples of schools trying to transform themselves from other researchers have added rich new illustrations of culture building. Even though we added new material, we wanted the book to be readable. It's short and contains engaging examples. We think readers will find the mix of stories interesting.

We focus on the elements of successful cultures and the ways leaders from every level—teachers, principals, parents, and community members—shape a school's cultural identity. Successful schools possess leaders who can read, assess, and reinforce core rituals, traditions, and values. Successful schools have leadership emanating from many people—leadership that maintains and supports learning for all students, as well as learning for staff. Successful cultures have leaders who know deep down in their hearts how important schools are to children and want to make them the best places they can be. Successful cultures have leaders who can cope with the paradoxes of their work and take advantage of the opportunities of the future. In this book, we hope to support, encourage, and nourish these kinds of leaders for schools.

Outline of the Book

We begin Chapter One by discussing the impact of culture on school achievement, change and reform, and student learning. Drawing on both organizational literature and research, we emphasize the importance of culture to achievement. Chapter Two presents a case study of a school that transformed itself by building a powerful, purposeful, and positive learning culture. The school, Ganado Primary, has visionary leadership, a deeply held purpose, rituals and traditions that support achievement, and celebrations that build commitment and motivation. Chapter Three turns to the importance of mission, purpose, and values in the culture. This chapter describes the importance of a meaningful purpose, positive norms, and deeply held values to add spark and vitality to the school. The power of purpose is illustrated in many examples. Chapter Four delves deeply into the relevance of rituals, traditions, and ceremonies in the school, as well as the benefit of the informal network to cultural health. Positive and negative examples of these features supply possibilities for leaders to ponder. Chapter Five turns to a look at the significance of past history and current stories to the stream of cultural energy. Central to any school culture is its history—the past events that have shaped the present. Equally important are the prevailing stories that permeate the school's consciousness and perpetuate important lessons. Leaders must attend to both the past and the present to shape a successful school. Chapter Six highlights the symbols of schools: architecture, mottoes, words, and actions. The ways leaders communicate purpose and build meaning symbolically are key to shaping successful cultures.

Chapter Seven illustrates, using new case examples, how leadership shapes culture in three schools. Chapter Eight describes the multiple roles that leaders take on in shaping the culture, including historian, anthropological sleuth, visionary, symbol, potter, poet, actor, and healer. The ways school leaders have enacted these roles are illustrated. Chapter Nine turns to cultural metamorphosis and transformation. Drawing on four case examples, we demonstrate how leadership can build school culture through consideration to purpose, energy, and all the elements of culture. Chapter Ten details a new conceptualization: toxic cultures. Drawing on extensive experience in schools and interviews with practitioners, we describe a variety of features that can be found in negative cultures or in the negative subcultures of positive schools. This chapter identifies features of the dark side of some school cultures and provides antidotes for some of these poisonous situations. Chapter Eleven examines the key relationship between the school and the community culture. Finally, Chapter Twelve turns to the challenges that leaders face in the future. We suggest that school leaders who want to build and maintain successful cultures will have to cope with paradox and take advantage of opportunities they confront. These paradoxes and challenges can shape the direction and hope for leaders in the next millennium.

Acknowledgments

The Deal-Peterson team has been around for several years. As with any duo, there are others around us who make substantial contributions to what we write. The first to receive our enduring thanks is Lee Bolman. He now teaches at the University of Missouri, Kansas City. His work with Terry Deal seeps into this book in a number of places. Thanks, Lee. You have one of the best conceptual minds in the business.

Thanks also to those whose work made this book possible; our administrative assistants Homa Aminmadani and Carole Jean Roche both put in hours and hours. We also express gratitude to our many graduate assistants—Valli Warren, Frances Wills, Kubilay Gok, and Nathaniel Bray—who have done a wonderful job chasing things down and pushing our ideas.

Over the years our colleagues Allan Kennedy, Sharon Conley, Linton Deck, Bob Slater, and Rick Ginsberg have influenced our thinking and clarity. Thanks also to students in our graduate and undergraduate classes and all the school leaders who have shared with us their stories, challenges, and successes. There is nothing like fresh minds and new blood combined with the wisdom of experience to enrich a book and get your ideas straight.

One colleague, Joan Vydra, deserves special mention. One of the most culturally attuned principals anywhere, she generously shared her experiences and solicited a number of contemporary cases. Thanks also to Gary Crow for helpful feedback on an earlier draft.

Our wives, Sandra Newport Deal and Ann Herrold-Peterson contributed love and support that helped fuel our creativity and energy. Our children—Kent's sons, Erik, Russell, and Scott, and Terry's daughter, Janie—have given us a real boost along the way.

We greatly appreciate the support and patience of Lesley Iura and Christie Hakim at Jossey-Bass.

We dedicate this work to the leaders of America's public schools. They can and do make a real difference in the lives of children. Keep the faith.

September 1998
Nashville, Tennessee   TERRENCE E. DEAL
Madison, Wisconsin   KENT D. PETERSON

The Authors

Terrence E. Deal's career has encompassed several roles, including that of police officer, teacher, principal, district office administrator, and professor. He has taught at the Stanford and Harvard Graduate Schools of Education and is now professor of educational leadership at Vanderbilt's Peabody College. He lectures and consults internationally with business, health care, educational, religious, and military organizations. He specializes in leadership, organizational theory and behavior, and culture. Deal is the coauthor of eighteen books, including *Corporate Cultures* (with Allan A. Kennedy, 1982)—an international best-seller. His most recent books are *Becoming a Teacher Leader* (with Lee Bolman, 1993), *The Leadership Paradox: Balancing Logic and Artistry in Schools* (with Kent D. Peterson, 1994), *Leading with Soul: An Uncommon Journey of Spirit* (with Lee Bolman, 1995), *Reframing Organizations: Artistry, Choice, and Leadership, Second Edition* (with Lee Bolman, 1997), and *Corporate Celebration: Play, Purpose, and Profit at Work* (with M. K. Key, 1998).

Kent D. Peterson was the first director of the Vanderbilt Principals' Institute and is former head of the National Center for Effective Schools Research and Development. He is currently professor in the Department of Educational Administration at the University of Wisconsin–Madison. He designs and consults in leadership academies across the United States and internationally. His research has examined the nature of principals' work, school reform, and the ways school leaders can develop effective educational settings. Author of numerous studies on principal leadership, he is coauthor of *The Principal's Role in Shaping School Culture* (with Terrence E. Deal, 1990) and *The Leadership Paradox: Balancing Logic and Artistry in Schools* (with Terrence E. Deal, 1994).

Shaping School Culture

1

Introduction

The Case for School Culture

"If only schools would behave more like businesses." It's a phrase we hear all too often. Its content haunts many school principals and teachers, often making them feel like they're missing something or following the wrong path. But let's take another look at the oft-invoked statement. What does it really mean? What makes successful businesses tick? Is it structure or strategy? Is it technology or clear goals?

The truth is probably deeper than these simple dichotomies suggest. But this much is clear: *The culture of an enterprise plays the dominant role in exemplary performance*. Highly respected organizations have evolved a shared system of informal folkways and traditions that infuse work with meaning, passion, and purpose.

Consider some well-known examples. Howard Schultz, CEO of Starbucks, puts it this way: "A company can grow big without losing the passion and personality that built it, but only if it's driven not by profits but by values and by people. . . . The key is heart. I pour my heart into every cup of coffee, and so do my partners at Starbucks. When customers sense that, they respond in kind. If you pour your heart into your work, or into any worthy enterprise, you can achieve dreams others may think impossible" (Schultz and Yang, 1997, p. 8).

Or step outside the business world and take a look at the U.S. Marine Corps. In his book *Making the Corps*, Thomas Ricks (1997) points to culture as the symbolic glue that has bonded the Corps together throughout its heralded military campaigns. He says, "Culture—that is, the values and assumptions that shape its members—is all the Marines have. It is what holds them together. They are the smallest of the U.S. military services, and in some ways the most interesting. Theirs is the richest culture: formalistic, insular, elitist, with a deep anchor in their own history and mythology" (p. 19).

There are countless other examples. The point is that if schools want to emulate other organizations, then parents, teachers, and administrators need to take a look at their local traditions and ways.

School Culture

The concept of schools having distinctive cultures is not new. Willard Waller wrote in 1932: "Schools have a culture that is definitely their own. There are, in the school, complex rituals of personal relationships, a set of folkways, mores, and irrational sanctions, a moral code based upon them. There are games, which are sublimated wars, teams, and an elaborate set of ceremonies concerning them. There are traditions, and traditionalists waging their world-old battle against innovators" (p. 96). His observations are still relevant in education today.

Parents, teachers, principals, and students have always sensed something special, yet undefined, about their schools—something extremely powerful but difficult to describe. This ephemeral, taken-for-granted aspect of schools is often overlooked and consequently is usually absent from discussions about school improvement. For decades the terms *climate* and *ethos* have been used to try to capture this powerful, pervasive, and notoriously elusive force. We believe the term *culture* provides a more accurate and intuitively appealing way to help school leaders better understand their school's own unwritten rules and traditions, norms, and expectations that seem to permeate everything: the way people act, how they dress, what they talk about or avoid talking about, whether they seek out colleagues for help or don't, and how teachers feel about their work and their students.

Beneath the conscious awareness of everyday life in schools, there is a stream of thought and activity. This underground flow of feelings and folkways wends its way within schools, dragging people, programs, and ideas toward often-unstated purposes: "This invisible, taken-for-granted flow of beliefs and assumptions gives meaning to what people say and do. It shapes how they interpret hundreds of daily transactions. This deeper structure of life in organizations is reflected and transmitted through symbolic language and expressive action. Culture consists of the stable, underlying social meanings that shape beliefs and behavior over time" (Deal and Peterson, 1990, p. 7).

The concept of culture has a long history in the exploration of human behavior across human groups. Anthropologists first developed the concept to explain differences among the all-encompassing life patterns of tribes, societies, and national or ethnic groups. Later, other social scientists applied the culture concept to the more limited aspects of patterns of behavior and thought within formal work organizations. Organizations usually have clearly distinguishable identities manifested in organizational members' patterns of behavior, thought, and norms. The concept of culture helps us understand these varied patterns—understand what they are, how they came to be, and how they affect performance.

Of the many different conceptions of culture, none is universally accepted as the one best definition. One scholar defines culture as the web of significance in which we are all suspended (Geertz, 1973). Another suggests simply that culture is "the way we do things around here" (Bower, 1966). Others define it as the shared beliefs and values that closely knit a community together (Deal and Kennedy, 1982).

Schein (1985) provides a widely recognized definition, calling it "a pattern of basic assumptions—invented, discovered, or developed by a given group as it learns to cope with problems . . . that has worked well enough to be considered valid and, therefore, to be taught to new members as the correct way to perceive, think, and feel in relation to those problems" (p. 9).

These complex entities do not develop overnight. In schools, for example, they are shaped by the ways principals, teachers, and key people reinforce, nurture, or transform underlying norms, values, beliefs, and assumptions.

School cultures are complex webs of traditions and rituals that have been built up over time as teachers, students, parents, and administrators work together and deal with crises and accomplishments (Schein, 1985; Deal and Peterson, 1990). Cultural patterns are highly enduring, have a powerful impact on performance, and shape the ways people think, act, and feel.

Culture and Productivity

In the business world, evidence is accumulating to show the significant role culture plays in financial performance. Let's also look at some recent studies.

Kotter and Heskett (1992) compared top-performing firms with less successful ones in the same business environment. They found that those with strong cultures attuned to prevailing business conditions outperformed their counterparts in several ways: revenue increased by an average of 682 percent compared to 166 percent; the workforce grew by 282 percent versus 36 percent; stock gained value by 901 percent contrasted with 74 percent; and income rose by 756 percent, eclipsing that of 1 percent in less cohesive firms.

Collins and Porras (1997) found similar results in their study of visionary companies—places where cultural values infused all aspects of everyday practice. They compared these visionary companies with other top-rated firms ("comparison companies" they called them) and with average performers. A look at the long-term financial performance of these three groups tells a dramatic story:

- Shareholders who, in 1926, invested $1 in the general stock market (average companies) would have accumulated $415 in growth and dividends by now.

- Shareholders who invested the same dollar in a more select portfolio (above-average companies) would have earned more than twice that amount—$955.

- Investors whose 1926 dollar was placed in visionary companies would today see a portfolio worth $6,356.

In the business world, culture stands out as a strong predictor of financial results. But does this same culture-performance link apply in education? Again, let's look at evidence.

In the late 1970s and early 1980s, the research on effective schools consistently showed that these schools had a climate and ethos that was purposeful and conducive to learning (Levine and Lezotte, 1990). These were places where a clear mission focused on student learning was embedded in a culture that supported high expectations for all students. The studies provided vivid proof of the power of culture.

In a landmark British study, Rutter and his colleagues (1979) established school "ethos" as a prime contributor to the academic achievement of students. Like other studies of successful schools, they discovered that the underlying norms, values, and traditions of a school contributed to achievement gains.

More recently, numerous studies of school change have identified the organizational culture as critical to the successful improvement of teaching and learning (Fullan, 1998; Rossman, Corbett, and Firestone, 1988). In study after study, where the culture did not support and encourage reform, that improvement did not occur. In contrast, improvement efforts were likely in schools where positive professional cultures had norms, values, and beliefs that reinforced a strong educational mission. Culture was a key factor in determining whether improvement was possible.

In a study that compared public and private schools, Bryk, Lee, and Holland (1993) found that a sense of community (very similar to our concept of culture) was a key factor in cultivating a sense of excellence in private schools. Teachers in these more communal schools were more satisfied with their work, seen by students as enjoying teaching, and less likely to be absent. Students in these schools were less likely to misbehave (for example, by cutting class, being absent, or disrupting class), were less likely to drop out, and showed higher gains in mathematic achievement. The researchers' conclusion is echoed in the work of Johnson (1990), who demonstrated the superior strength and cohesion of culture in private schools relative to their public counterparts.

McLaughlin (1995), in a longitudinal study, found tremendous variation in schools, even departments, serving similar populations. For example, a school with 80 percent Latino students (School A) and a school with 80 percent African American students (School B) demonstrated strikingly different levels of performance, even though they served students from comparable backgrounds. School A had a drop-out rate of 60 percent between the ninth and twelfth grades. Most grades fell in the D or F range, with very few As. Only 20 percent of the students went on to acquire higher education. Teachers were heard to lament their fate in having to work in the school. In School B, students scored in the top quartile in mathematics, scored first in the district in language arts, and showed up well in music and the performing arts. By all measures this was a top-performing school. The difference, according to McLaughlin, was that School B had a teacher-learning community. It was a place of cohesion, passion, commitment, and extensive interactions among teachers. The higher-performing school had a positive, focused culture.

An extensive study of school restructuring showed conclusively that changing the structure of schools is not enough (Newmann and Associates, 1996). To have success, both new structures and a professional culture are needed. In this five-year study, the researchers found that school success flourished in cultures with a primary focus on student learning, a commitment to high expectations, social support for innovation, dialogue, and the search for new ideas. Also present was an "ethos of caring, sharing, and mutual help among staff, and between staff and students, based on respect, trust, and shared power relations among staff" (p. 289). Other investigations of all types have demonstrated the significance of school culture to school success.

Functions and Impact of Culture

School culture affects every part of the enterprise from what faculty talk about in the lunch room, to the type of instruction that is valued, to the way professional development is viewed, to the importance of learning for all students. Strong, positive, collaborative cultures have powerful effects on many features of schools. Several examples follow.

Culture fosters school effectiveness and productivity (Purkey and Smith, 1983; Levine and Lezotte, 1990; Newmann and Associates, 1996). Teachers can succeed in a culture focused on productivity (rather than on maintenance or ease of work), performance (hard work, dedication, perseverance), and improvement (continuous fine-tuning and refinement of teaching). Such a culture helps teachers overcome the uncertainty of their work (Lortie, 1975) by providing focus and collegiality. It provides social motivation to persevere in the demanding work of teaching thirty children in a small space. It encourages, sanctions, and rewards the professionals' constant task of improving their craft.

Culture improves collegial and collaborative activities that foster better communication and problem-solving practices (Little, 1982; Peterson and Brietzke, 1994). In school cultures valuing collegiality and collaboration, there is a better climate for the social and professional exchange of ideas, the enhancement and spread of effective practices, and widespread professional problem solving.

Culture fosters successful change and improvement efforts (Little, 1982; Louis and Miles, 1990; Deal and Peterson, 1990). Toxic cultures that support mediocrity, inertia, and apathy are not likely to be innovative. In contrast, in schools that embrace norms of performance, change, and efficacy, staff gladly experiment with new approaches, seek innovative practices to solve enduring problems, and reinforce a learning-focused vision for the school. A school's culture encourages learning and progress by fostering a climate of purposeful change, support for risk taking and experimentation, and a community spirit valuing purposeful progress.

Culture builds commitment and identification of staff, students, and administrators (Schein, 1985). People are motivated and feel committed to an organization that has meaning, values, and an ennobling purpose. Commitment grows in strong, caring social cultures. Identification is strengthened with a clear and crystallized mission that is inspiring and deeply held. Motivation is strengthened through rituals that nurture identification, traditions that intensify connection to the school, and ceremonies that build community.

Culture amplifies the energy, motivation, and vitality of a school staff, students, and community. It has long been known that the social climate and culture of a school influence the emotional and psychological orientation of its staff. As many say, the "context is infectious." This is especially the case in schools that are optimistic, socially caring and supportive, and energetic. Staff, students, and community are likely to take on those same characteristics and become positive, energized, caring, and encouraging. But the opposite is true as well. Some school cultures are "toxic." The social milieu is so negative that even the positive individual can become discouraged or disheartened.

Culture increases the focus of daily behavior and attention on what is important and valued (Deal and Kennedy, 1982; Schein, 1985). Although rules, job descriptions, and policies can shape what a person does, the unwritten rules, the informal expectations, and rites and rituals of daily life may be even more meaningful harbingers of action and sustained progress. These unstated, often hidden assumptions and expectations are embedded in cultural patterns and become more intensified over time. With strong and meaningful values, daily work is focused on the important issues of quality instruction, continuous refinement of teaching, and the accelerated learning of all students.

Symbolic Leadership

With all the evidence from both business and education highlighting culture as a critical aspect of organizational cohesion and performance, what's holding us back? Why do standards and restructuring continue to play such a dominant role in educational improvement and reform? Part of the explanation lies in the way we look at educational organizations.

Bolman and Deal (1997) have identified four lenses, or "frames," that people rely on to frame, assess, and respond to situations. First, a *human resource* frame emphasizes people's needs, skills, and the importance of a caring, trusting climate. Next, the *structural* frame emphasizes goals, efficiency, policies, a clear chain of command, and results. Third, the *political* frame highlights a world of scarce resources, power, conflict, negotiations, and compromise. Finally, the *symbolic* frame focuses attention on meaning and the symbols, rituals, ceremonies, stories, or other symbolic forms in which faith and hope are encompassed and communicated.

In the world of education, some lenses are more prominent than others. For example, policymakers rely very heavily on the structural frame in developing mandates for school reform. Nearly all the reform initiatives of the past three decades have emphasized goals, standards, restructuring, or similar changes. Conversely, school leaders—teachers and principals—tend to read and respond to day-to-day challenges from the human resource frame. Although some principals (especially in high schools) and superintendents may be more structurally oriented, the human resource lens is common at all school levels. Although politics is disdained publicly as distasteful or pathological, people still use power and influence behind the scenes to get what they want. Finally, the symbolic and cultural side of schools is too often viewed as "soft" or as a superficial afterthought.

This neglect of the symbolic aspect of schools does not square with ideas of what successful leadership is all about. One of the most significant roles of leaders (and of leadership) is the creation, encouragement, and refinement of the symbols and symbolic activity that give meaning to the organization. The late Lou Pondy (1976), sociologist of business organizations, points out that the effectiveness of a leader is in the ability to make actions meaningful to others.

Edgar Schein (1985), an organizational psychologist, states the case for cultural leadership even more forcefully. He says that "there is a possibility underemphasized in leadership research, that the only thing of real importance that leaders do is to create and manage culture and that the unique talent of leaders is their ability to work with culture" (p. 2).

In this book we will examine the ways leaders shape culture, creating cohesive places that help teachers teach and students learn. Leaders in strong cultures are everywhere—teachers, administrators, parents, even students. Together these leaders read, shape, and continuously transform the culture of their school.

Schools' Need for Improvement

There is widespread consensus that America's schools need significant improvement. The idea that schools should behave more like businesses is also frequently expressed. But when we consider what those improvements should be and how we should go about making them, the shared consensus turns to sharp disagreement. We think the schools should, in fact, behave more like businesses. But our reasons for that are different from the ones usually given.

Our reason: *Top businesses have developed a shared culture*. A successful company's culture pumps meaning, passion, and purpose into the enterprise. Company leaders know that success flourishes only when people are committed, believe in the organization, and take pride in their work. These places of work become beloved institutions where people pour their heart and soul into everyday ritual and routine.

The same must become true of our nation's schools. While values, folkways, and traditions will take form reflecting the unique character of educational institutions, the human side of good organizations may be worth emulating. In education, the risk of not doing things right is even higher. A poor-quality product or service can be recycled, but a young person who does not learn or who drops out is hard to salvage—a lost treasure. Top-drawer teaching and learning can never flourish in a sterile or toxic environment.

The evidence is persuasive. The challenge is real. The need for some leaders to step forward and take the necessary risks to build positive school cultures has never been greater. If Starbucks' CEO can pour his heart into a cup of coffee, so too can school leaders pour their hearts into student learning.

Part I

Elements of Culture

2

Schools as Tribes

The tiny town of Ganado is in the high desert of Northern Arizona. It is situated in the midst of an expansive and beautiful reservation twenty-seven miles from Window Rock—the largest city in Navajo lands. This is picturesque country, dry and beautiful, dotted with traditional hogans and small homes. To outsiders, the town of Ganado would be one of the last places expected to house an award-winning elementary school. The town has one of the highest unemployment rates in the country. Forty-six percent of the families do not have running water, and 35 percent have no access to electricity across the district's one thousand square miles. Despite the odds, Ganado Primary School is the town's pride and joy and is nationally recognized for its excellence.

A Desert Jewel: Ganado Primary School

The school is a large, modern building that is centrally located and visible from the main road and from the town. Its color blends with the history and spirit of the community. Its entry courtyard features a smaller likeness of Spider Rock—a spiritually significant, eight-hundred-foot vertical sandstone pinnacle rising from Canyon de Chelly. The sculpture beckons students to enter a way of life.

The school was not always a source of community pride. Some years ago, Ganado Primary was identified as having one of the worst school buildings in Arizona. Building the new school was the beginning of a new identity: a distinctive set of cultural ways and practices that are anchored in tradition but embrace modern standards. The school's culture now envelops students as they go about the business of growing and learning.

A walk through the school reveals a symbolic picture of the school's cultural values and assumptions. Upon entering the school, a visitor sees an inviting, open area that is dominated by the Spider Rock. More than mere adornment, the replica represents a sacred time in Navajo history. According to tradition, this is where Spider Woman gave the Navajo the knowledge of weaving. Today, the entry-way spire christens Ganado Primary as a historically anchored, sacred place to gain knowledge.

Inside the school is a fusion of modern educational equipment and methods with symbols of the traditional ways of the Navajo people. For example, the school is configured in four units, each denoting one of the tribe's four sacred directions. Each direction represents a core value of the Navajo people. Each section houses a team of teachers and a cohort of students.

Other features also reinforce cultural values. For example, the library is located in the center of the building. It displays thousands of books in open view as students move from one part of the school to another. Hallways are airy and light. A room used for meetings, reflection, and community gatherings is shaped in the form of a hogan—an ancient and specially shaped Navajo home. Traditional wooden posts holding up the ceiling seem perfectly in harmony with modern paraphernalia: books, computers, scanners, camcorders, and VCRs.

Hallways are adorned with Navajo rugs that are woven in the characteristic Ganado red geometric design favored by local weavers. Student work is displayed everywhere. In the front hall is a display case housing awards won by the school, book bags given to teachers each year during staff development sessions, and school t-shirts designed by students.

Architecture and artifacts vividly represent the school's core values and basic beliefs as embodied in the school's mission statement:

> The Ganado Primary School's mission is to provide opportunities for children to make sense of their world, to respect themselves and others, to respect their environment, and to appreciate and understand their cultural and linguistic heritage. Children, teachers and administrators all bring varying points of view, resources, expectations of and assumptions about the world, and ways of dealing with their daily circumstances. Our mission is to help everyone negotiate their experiences with the content of the classroom, instructional style, and the social, emotional, physical and professional interactions of school life. We believe that a relaxed atmosphere where surprise, challenge, hard work, celebration, humor, satisfaction and collegiality is the natural order of the day for all.
>
> Care must be taken to insure that sound philosophical, developmental and cultural understandings of children are at the heart of decision making in the classroom and the school. The question, "What is it like to be a child?" underlies staff development, matters of curriculum, parent involvement and instructional approaches. "What is it like to be a teacher?" is an equally valid question. What is true about our mission to children is true for teachers and staff as well.

The school's cultural values are also evident in the principal's poem about his own values. Written in 1997 by Sigmund Boloz, the poem on the next page gives a portrait of his core obligations.

THE C DIET

My job is:

to keep the compass
to massage change
to build credibility: a positive image for the school in the eyes of
    the community
to cultivate my staff
to ask the compelling questions
to be an advocate for children
I build the culture of the school

    curriculum   consensus   constituents   community

I see my job as building my staff. I strive to build:

confidence in themselves, in their decisions and in their teaching
courage to take risks and to break new ground
compassion for children and others
character to always do their personal best

competence that they know the current trends
capacity to learn new things
commitment to our mission
clarity a good focus on the whats and the hows
consciousness to bring thinking to a higher level

communication open lines of dialog
collaboration share expertise
connectedness bonding to each other and our mission
collegiality professional interactions

challenge to keep staff on their cutting edge
critical thinking thoughtfulness
creativity to implement innovations
curiosity actively seek better ways
contentment feel accepted

Ganado's Mission and Rituals

The school's mission and purpose cast a shadow far beyond the written word. The school year is filled with rituals, traditions, and ceremonies that reinforce core values and beliefs.

Four times a year, a "Once Upon a Time Breakfast" invites students, teachers, and parents to bring their favorite books and celebrate literacy while they enjoy food and drink. Students are regularly acknowledged for their growth and learning. During a "Celebrating Quality Learning Award Ceremony," sometimes up to a quarter of the students receive some award for writing, quality work, citizenship, dance, or drama, or for work in the Navajo language. Parents and teachers sit with the children and celebrate together what they have all done well.

Parents' learning also prevails at Ganado, with parent workshops on important topics, a series of year-long general education degree (GED) workshops, and frequent celebration of their learning and accomplishments.

Every Tuesday, the principal meets with teachers from one of the four units for a "curriculum conversation." They explore new ideas by discussing articles or books, viewing videotapes or new approaches, or observing individual teaching approaches. The dialogue and collaborative learning offers new perspectives on curriculum, instruction, and learning. As the principal says, "I cannot allow a teacher to stop growing. You need to be thinking, learning, be a model in your class."

Child-focused curriculum innovation is also stimulated through voluntary focus groups that identify a topic to be investigated in-depth. For example, ten teachers might examine how to teach poetry; another group might discuss first-grade writing. These gatherings occur from 11 A.M. until 1 P.M. Classes are covered for all who wish to participate. The meetings are lively, focused, and collegial, building skills and a sense of community at the same time.

An "Early Childhood Academy" is held each year for classroom aides to provide ideas and convey a sense of importance to paraprofessionals in the school. They are immersed for a full week in early childhood concepts and classroom techniques. All participants receive book bags with the academy name and year prominently displayed, symbolizing their responsibility to carry their newfound knowledge back to the classroom.

As the principal notes: "We marinate students in literacy and activities in the classroom. And we marinate our staff in new ideas, new dialogues, new approaches."

Another staff ritual is "Teachers as Readers," providing time for teachers to eat together and talk about what they are reading. Staff bring a new book or article that they want to share, discuss, consider.

The Tourguide Program is a relatively new tradition in the school. First- and second-grade students take the more than seven hundred visitors a year around the school, pointing out student work, community weavers, and school awards. These youthful guides become both purveyors and consumers of their own culture and history.

Staff members, the principal, and those in the community regularly recount stories that bring the school to life. They tell stories of change and renewal, as the school was transformed from one of the worst to one of the best in Arizona. They share stories of the many conferences and training programs that have filled their school with new ideas, new instructional approaches, and new levels of achievement. They tell stories of the parents who once felt excluded and outsiders who now work in the school, get their GEDs, and come to early-childhood conferences. The stories are all about reaching goals, overcoming obstacles, learning by everyone, and working together as a community.

The informal network at Ganado Primary is filled with role models. The school superintendent—distant and authoritarian in other places—is seen as a special person at Ganado. A Navajo, he has been there for thirty years; those who know him think he has a good heart; some say perhaps he cares too much. When he visits the school, children come up to talk with him, or they write him through the school post office—and he responds. Then there is Grandma Taliman, a foster grandparent for many children. This older person from the community visits with staff and children, bringing attention and caring that only the elderly can offer. She makes people feel good just by being a quiet, understanding, and kind person.

The four units of the school become tight-knit family subcultures. They often have breakfast and lunch together; curriculum conversations occur within these units, and teachers take special pride in "their kids." Each cluster is seen as its own small neighborhood, and students feel connected and cared for.

Against heavy odds, Ganado Primary is succeeding through a tightly woven, meaningful system of historically anchored cultural traditions and values. The school's purpose is reflected in artifacts and architecture, embodied in core values and beliefs, reinforced through ritual and ceremony, carried through stories and lore, and watched over by an informal group of players. School leadership abounds in the building. These are the set of elements—the building blocks—that every school assembles to build a cohesive culture that gives purpose, vitality, and direction to an effective educational enterprise. School cultures—no matter whom they serve—become like tribes and clans, with deep ties among people and with values and traditions that give meaning to everyday life. In the next chapters, we explore the elements of culture in more detail.

3

Vision and Value
The Bedrock of Culture

Where did we come from? Why are we here? Where are we going? What do we hold as sacred? What importance does our work have? What lessons do we wish to pass from generation to generation? These questions fall under the rubric of mythology.

Myths in Organizations

Every human group anchors its existence in a unifying myth that orients the group's worldview. Schools with strong cultures are no different. This unifying myth details how the group came to be, why it exists, and what it holds most dear. The long history of a school and its deeper sense of purpose and direction are included in its myth.

This mythic side of a school is the story behind the story. Myth sits at the center of what life in the school is all about. It looms as a school's existential anchor—its spiritual source, the wellspring of cultural traditions and ways. We will use such concepts as mission, purpose, values, and beliefs to approximate the meaning behind the myth—to get to the deeper level of what life in schools is really all about.

Mission and Purpose in Schools

At the heart of a school's culture are its mission and purpose—the focus of what people do. Although not easy to define, mission and purpose instill the intangible forces that motivate teachers to teach, school leaders to lead, children to learn, and parents and the community to have confidence in their school. Mission and purpose shape definitions of success (Schein, 1985)—definitions that vary from school to school.

The struggle to come to terms with mission and purpose is often manifested in mission or vision statements. These are attempts to get to the core of what a school seeks to realize—its sacred mission or ennobling purpose. But in attempts to reach for this deeper mythical level, too often schools produce abstract documents that have little to do with what really matters or what people do on a day-to-day basis. In a larger urban high school, for example, the assembled staff was asked to describe the school mission. After a long silence, the principal replied, "It's written on the wall outside the auditorium—our school philosophy." A request for someone to tell what was on the wall resulted in silence.

But mission and purpose always run deep. People need a medium that will help people connect with the school's reason for existence.

Purpose and Definitions of Success

Definitions of success, as Schein (1985) notes, reflect the purposes of schools and vary from place to place. They can emphasize some of the following:

Achieving extracurricular success. In some schools, how well the football team does is a central focus of what makes a successful year. As is so vividly detailed in the now-classic *Friday Night Lights* (Bissinger, 1991), a school and its community can be obsessed with winning in athletic contests. The myth and purpose of the school reside in the Friday night football games. This same emphasis can also carry over to the performance of the school band (Our band has been in the Macy's Thanksgiving Day Parade three times!) or other extracurricular activities (The school yearbook has won highest honors five years running!). In some schools, emphasis on athletics or other activities outshines academic success.

Performing well. Some schools value teaching. Success is achieved when teachers believe they have done a good job. If their lesson or presentation is well organized, they feel successful. Sometimes, however, these teachers are great presenters or engaging speakers—sages on stage—but students may learn best in a different modality. Great performances can fall on deaf ears. When students don't learn in these classrooms, they too often receive blame. Good teaching is successful only when students learn.

Learning for the elite. In some schools, success is measured by the number of students accepted at Ivy League colleges or designated as National Merit Scholars. The culture focuses on the success of top students. One school felt a sense of accomplishment when the staff produced double-digit numbers of National Merit Scholars (at least ten in the year). In reaching this pinnacle of success, however, the needs of many other students were ignored. Students who are not part of the elite lose motivation, as staff spend most of their time and energy devising new strategies to serve the needs of the highest-performing students.

Surviving, or not making waves. Some schools define success as getting by, surviving another day, week, or year. The emphasis is on not making waves or becoming too visible. Staff are happy when they are left alone. The cultural focus on just getting by influences students. They know that if they're not a bother, they'll be promoted and graduated.

Embracing the new flavor of the month. For some schools, success is defined as being first with the latest. Instituting a new instructional approach, using new technology, or trying whatever currently is in vogue is what counts. It doesn't matter whether students learn. What is more important is that something innovative is in the works. Change itself becomes the shared mission.

Learning for all students. Some schools give their heart and soul to seeking high standards of learning for all students. In these cultures teachers focus on the learning needs of everyone, from the most highly succeeding to the furthest behind. Time and attention is spent working on the improvement of learning—across the board. Celebrations are convened when all students succeed. Success is defined by how many students reach their learning potential.

Different missions and purposes define outcomes that are valued and shape how energy and time are allocated by staff, students, and administrators. Purpose and mission do many things for schools. For example, they define what actions ought to occur; they motivate staff and students by signaling what is important and what will be rewarded; and they steer the allocation and distribution of resources, depending on what is considered important or valuable.

Values, Beliefs, Assumptions, and Norms

Mission and purpose give guidance to what people work toward on a daily and weekly basis. Other concepts used to capture the deep mythical underpinning of school culture include assumptions, values, beliefs, and norms. Each is a related, often overlapping, way to get at the sacred calling of an educational enterprise. Sometimes used interchangeably with mission and purpose, each has a special contribution to make in capturing the symbolic glue that holds a school together.

Values are the conscious expressions of what an organization stands for. Values define a standard of goodness, quality, or excellence that undergirds behavior and decision making, and what people care about (Ott, 1989). Values are not simply goals or outcomes; values are a deeper sense of what is important. Without an existential commitment, everything is relative; values focus attention and define success.

Beliefs are how we comprehend and deal with the world around us. They are "consciously held, cognitive views about truth and reality" (Ott, 1989, p. 39). Beliefs originate in group and personal experiences and through reading books and articles. Beliefs are powerful in schools because they represent the core understandings about student capacity (immutable or alterable), teacher responsibility for learning (little or a lot), expert sources of teacher knowledge (experience, research, or intuition), and educational success (will never happen or is achievable).

Assumptions are sometimes viewed as the preconscious "system of beliefs, perceptions, and values" that guide behavior (Ott, 1989). They are deeply embedded in the cultural tapestry, and they shape thoughts and actions in powerful ways. A school may have underlying assumptions about certain types of children (either that they can't learn or that they always do), about the nature of teaching (it's an art or a craft), or about the nature of curriculum (it's a sequential body of knowledge or a set of central issues). Cultural assumptions are hard to assess because they are so closely aligned with myths.

Norms consolidate assumptions, values, and beliefs. They are unstated group expectations for behavior, dress, and language. These prescriptions become "behavioral blueprints" that people are supposed to follow; they are "organizational sea anchors providing predictability and stability" (Ott, 1989, p. 37). Norms develop formally and informally as the staff in a school discover and reinforce particular ways of acting and interacting. They are bolstered by messages and sanctions when individuals overstep the normative bounds.

In some schools, for example, norms govern what teachers are expected to wear (jeans or dresses), how one treats parents (as enemies or as collaborators), what one should talk about during prep periods (new cars or instruction), and how often a teacher should attend workshops on instruction (seldom or often).

Positive norms vary from school to school. Kilmann (1985), Saphier and King (1985), and Deal and Peterson (1994) have identified *positive norms* that are found in schools, including the following:

Treat people with respect.

See everyone as a potential source of valuable insights and
expertise.

Be willing to take on responsibilities.

Try to initiate changes to improve performance.

Encourage those who suggest new ideas.

Be conscious of costs.

Speak with pride about the school and your unit.

Allocate time according to the importance of the tasks.

Don't criticize the school in front of students or community.

Enjoy and be enthusiastic in your work.

Be helpful and supportive of the others in the school.

Share information to make the organization better.

Do what will serve the needs of students rather than what will
serve personal needs only.

But negative, dysfunctional norms exist in some schools. These
same researchers have identified *dysfunctional norms* that might
occur in schools, including the following:

Don't disagree with the principal.

Don't make waves.

Treat women as inferior.

Put your school down.

Hate your work.

Hide new ideas and information from others.

Treat colleagues poorly.

Look busy and innovative when you're not.

Reward or recognize others on the basis of politics.

Laugh at and criticize those who are innovative.

Complain and criticize your school to the outside.

Complain constantly about everything.

Distrust colleagues.

Share information only when it benefits your own unit.

Do what will serve personal needs first and the needs of students later.

Ignore areas of curriculum, instruction, and learning that are problematic; rationalize why they can't get better.

Identifying the positive and negative norms is a key task of school leaders, one we will turn to shortly.

Remystification of Schools

Every school chooses its language to capture its deep-seated cultural commitments. Some focus on ennobling purpose and sacred mission. Some review and reinforce important assumptions. Others try to consolidate and communicate core values and beliefs. Still others stand back and take a look at unstated norms that may help or hinder the educational process.

Whatever the route to meeting objectives, the questions are the same: How do we recapture the magic and myth of education? How do we restore a mythology that enables teachers to believe in their importance and convince the public that schools are worthy of their confidence and support? Some believe the path to these ends is rational, in other words that seeing is believing. Show people results and they will once again have faith in schools. We advocate another direction—that believing is seeing. How do we reinvigorate the culture of schools so that teachers believe in themselves and the public rediscovers the hope it once had?

The key here lies in the culture of schools—the shared meaning these institutions create. The bedrock of cultural vitality and stability lies in the mission, purpose, values, beliefs, assumptions, and norms that people share. Some reformers in recent memory have concentrated on the demystification of schools: to get better, make them more rational. We and other writers see another possibility, that is, to re-embrace the mythology that launched the public school system in this country: school should be a place to create a sense of community; each student should be able to realize his or her potential; each student has promise; each student can become a greater American.

Restructuring or setting new standards will not achieve the level of success that reformers hope for without remystifying and reculturing schools and classrooms.

4

Ritual and Ceremony

Culture in Action

Imagine our lives without ritual and ceremony. Do away with morning coffee, the noon lunch break, the evening social hour, the late-night walking of the dog, or whatever the special breaks are that you look forward to each day. It's a chilling thought; our daily or weekly rituals provide a welcome chance to reflect and connect. We renew ourselves, bond with others, and experience life's deeper meaning in our everyday liturgy. Think of the hollowness we would create if we were to cancel Halloween, Thanksgiving, Christmas, Cinco de Mayo, Hanukkah, Kwanzaa, Easter, Passover, summer picnics, or New Year's Eve. Without ceremony to honor traditions, mark the passage of time, graft reality and dreams onto old roots, or reinforce our cherished values and beliefs, our very existence could become empty, sterile, and devoid of meaning. Without ritual and ceremony, any culture will wither and die. Without periodic expressive events, nothing makes much sense and we lose our way.

Ritual and ceremony allow us to act out what otherwise is hard to touch and comprehend. In doing so, we touch base with our core values and bond with each other. Ritual and ceremony are to culture what the movie is to the script, the concert is to the score, or the dance is to values difficult to express in any other way (Deal and Kennedy, 1982).

Now shift from our personal lives to life in the organizations where we work. Imagine school without such symbolic interludes.

In the world of education with its multiple challenges and complex goals, ritual is probably more important than in a business with a tangible product or service. Schools run largely on faith and hope. Students and teachers don't leave their humanity behind when they come to school. They need special moments in the daily grind to reflect on what's really important, to connect with one another, and to feel the common spirit that makes technical routine more like spiritual communion.

In the past few decades, in the name of educational reform, we have managed to sterilize schools of the symbolic acts that help culture survive and thrive. Some ritual and ceremony has fallen victim to political correctness. Some has been dismissed as fluff in favor of structure and rationality. A lot has just been overlooked and ignored, allowed to wither away. More than ever, we need to revive ritual and ceremony as the spiritual fuel we need to energize and put more life back into our schools. Learning is fostered in large part by strong traditions, frequent ritual, and poignant ceremonies to reinvigorate cultural cohesion and focus.

Rituals

Rituals are procedures or routines that are infused with deeper meaning. They help make common experiences uncommon events. Every school has hundreds of routines, from the taking of attendance in the morning to the exiting procedures used in the afternoon. But when these routine events can be connected to a school's mission and values, they summon spirit and reinforce cultural ties.

Let's look at a couple of examples. In one rural midwestern school, food service workers make toast for staff and students every morning—even though it's not in their official job description. As a routine it feeds people and provides carbohydrates and calories, but as a ritual of "breaking bread" together, it energizes the communal spirit for the coming day. A recent attempt to eliminate the morning ritual failed, as hundreds of past students,

staff, and parents recalled the fond memories and wanted the tradition to continue.

In a large urban school, staff meet for coffee and doughnuts once
a week to share stories about their experiences with new curriculum
ideas and to renew relationships and recharge batteries with colleagues they see only occasionally.

Rituals become significant traditional events with special history and meaning. The tradition unfolds year in and year out. Traditions provide a vital tie to the past, reinvigorate the present, and
offer a welcome promissory note for a robust future. Special events
touch the hearts of parents and others in the community who can
recall with feeling their own experiences in school. When people
honor traditional rituals, it gives them a cultural foundation to
weather challenges, difficulties, and change. Rituals are the daily
comings and goings that create the mortar that binds people and
activities; rituals hold a school together.

Schools have a variety of rituals that do culture's symbolic work:

*Greeting and goodbye rituals are value-embedded ways of connecting
people.* At Audubon Elementary School the workroom is filled with
teachers each morning, and greetings are boisterous, usually taking
place over homemade treats. At Ganado Primary, newcomers to the
school are taken around by an articulate Navajo tour guide who
shows them student work, rugs from local weavers, and awards the
school has received. In a Beaverton, Oregon, elementary school the
official greeting of teachers and students is an animated "high five"—
a behavioral testimony to the school's commitment to "Reach for
Excellence." Bob Herring, the principal of Nativity School who is
described in Case 2 at the end of the chapter, uses deep rituals to
greet and to say goodbye to students and staff.

*Transition rituals provide the symbolic support to bridge changes in
practice or procedures.* In one school where more traditional textbooks had given way to trade books in language arts, the staff gathered to remember the good and the ridiculous about the texts. They

were then boxed up and sent to a needy traditional school in another state. In another school, older technologies—from pens to Pentiums—are placed in a special cabinet to show the progression of technology used in the school.

Battle preparation rituals gird staff and students with the needed armor to face threatening challenges. In one school just before the state-mandated tests are given, staff and students gather around an enormous cake that has "We Will Succeed" written in huge letters across the top. This ritual prepares staff and students to do their best in the face of a challenging, high-stakes examination. In another school, teachers and administrators fill care baskets with cards, notes, stuffed animals, and other small items when teachers are facing graduate exams or other stress-filled times.

Initiation rituals connect newcomers to a school's community. These rituals can be as simple as a significant introduction of a staff member's past successes and special attributes at the first faculty meeting. Or they can be more complex: meaningful mentoring relationships that involve reflection on professional values and philosophy, shared group participation at commonly attended conferences, and extensive discussions on the history and core values of the school. In a New York elementary school, the old-timers—veteran teachers who have been at the school for an extended period—take over the newcomers' staff development. They share the school's history and traditions. As the principal observed of the rite's impact: "It's worked both for the newcomers and old-timers. The only thing worse than not learning the ropes is having great traditions to share but no audience of initiates."

Closing rituals furnish the needed support and compassion when things end. In one elementary school, teachers and students create "Big Books" featuring the year's special events, surprises, and accomplishments. Poems, pictures, and stories fill the history that is ceremonially placed in the library. As we describe shortly, the Nativity School cements ties and copes with endings by recognizing the contributions people have made to the school and releasing balloons into the spring sky.

Rituals are the daily interactions that are infused with meaning. Ceremonies are larger, more complex social gatherings that build meaning and purpose.

Ceremonies

Most schools have some formal ceremonies that mark transitions in the school year. These periodic events bind people to each other and shape unwritten cultural values and rules. The traditions shape and mold new recruits and give seasoned staff a welcome spiritual boost.

Ceremonies are complex, culturally sanctioned ways that a school celebrates successes, communicates its values, and recognizes special contributions of staff and students. Each season of the year can provide time to communicate ceremonially the deeper symbolic glue that binds a school together. In an urban school, before classes start in the fall, staff gather together to share their hopes, ideas, and dreams for the coming year. This shared experience creates connections that last throughout the year, despite the predictable ups and downs of the academic calendar.

In another school the staff hold a special art night; each student has a piece of artwork matted and displayed. Parents and community members are invited to appreciate students' creativity. Special awards are given to parents and others in recognition of their cooperation and help. The contribution of teachers is singled out for special attention in the carefully and artistically designed brochure that outlines the evening's festivities. This ceremony knits a diverse community together in celebration of the collective successes of children. It builds, bonds, and cements organizational esteem.

In another school, staff hold an end-of-the-year ceremony to recognize the individual and group contributions of teachers. In sometimes funny and sometimes serious ways, the school communicates how it values the ways teachers work together.

Types of Ceremonies

Schools with unique cultures convene ceremonies for several purposes during the year:

Opening-day ceremonies rebind staff to the school and its mission. These events reinforce core values, remind people of the hard yet rewarding year ahead, and celebrate their commitment to the growth of young people. In one school, staff and parents represented on the school's council come together for a beginning-of-school potluck. Each person brings a dish that represents something they did over the summer—Texas chili from a parent who attended a summer conference in Houston or an Irish stew from a teacher whose summer was devoted to developing a new teaching module on immigration. Eating good food and trying to "read" the food's deeper meaning creates fun times and renews ties for the coming year.

Community renewal ceremonies revive connections and reinforce shared values. These special events can rebuild and recharge the energies of staff and students as well as parents. Beginning a new school year always conjures both anticipation and dread. Educating students is a complex and daunting task. Renewal ceremonies can build trust and faith to face the year's next 180 days. At one school, for example, the mission statement is reviewed each fall. It is refined or reworded to match current values. Then the statement is redone in a new calligraphy by a local artist and signed by everyone. This makes the mission statement alive, vital, connected to everyday experience, and evolving, rather than one that's dead, moribund, and gathering dust as it hangs on a wall.

Seasonal ceremonies take advantage of cyclical celebrations outside the school. Reitzug and Reeves (1992) found in one school that the principal, Mr. Sage, has a Thanksgiving tradition in which he cooks and serves a large turkey, using the activity to teach about weights and measures but also to renew teachers in the middle of the first semester.

Management ceremonies ease the hard work of formulating plans and deciding on new programs. Professionals often gather and make improvement plans through brute force of rationality. But infusing these times with a collaborative spirit and shared collegiality fosters even greater accomplishment. A Kentucky high school working to restructure its educational program held its planning retreats at the principal's rustic cabin. The principal, a strong and insightful leader, knew the importance of shared thinking and planning. But she also recognized the other side of the equation. She cooked incredible food and encouraged play as the core planning council hammered out new directions. They often referred to their gatherings as "an advance" rather than a "retreat." In a Connecticut school, it was not a rustic cabin but a hotel with a reputation for lavish buffets that made the planning retreat a meaningful group tradition.

Integrative ceremonies provide ways to meld the various social, ethnic, and religious groups in a school. As schools become more and more diverse ethnically, socially, and economically, they need to rediscover or invent traditions that knit people together—integrative traditions that help everyone develop understanding and appreciation for others. At Piccolo Elementary School in Chicago, African American students learn Spanish songs to sing during Cinco de Mayo; Hispanic students learn rap to participate during African-American-week festivities. These are more than music lessons, as students develop friendships and learn about different values and ways. In the Tucson, Arizona, school district, opening day brought all its employees together to kick off the new year. At various places in the large arena, student groups were featured playing ethnic music. The music helped unite diverse subgroups into a shared commitment to building a cohesive learning community.

Recognition ceremonies pay tribute to the special accomplishments of individuals and groups, thereby forging pride and respect. Schools, like other organizations, too often avoid recognizing and celebrating important accomplishments. Sometimes it is not part of tradition; quite often, negative members of the culture want to diminish praise to hide their own mediocrity. But successful cultures find ways—both small and elaborate ways—to celebrate, commemorate, and salute the accomplishments of others. For the school, this heightens the feeling of being on a winning team, of being part of something greater than themselves.

In the Beaverton Elementary School mentioned earlier, the daily "high-five" rites are supplemented from time to time by a special recognition event. Teachers, students, and parents gather in the school's "hall of fame" to recognize those who have shown notable merit in "reaching for excellence." The principal calls a student forward, reads the accomplishment, and paints the student's hand. The student slaps the wall with a high-five, leaving an imprint. The principal then writes the student's name and his or her accomplishment.

There are many other examples of this recognition: student awards ceremonies, volunteer lunches, graduation ceremonies, and honor roll dinners. At Joyce Elementary in Detroit, students who make the honor roll attend a formal ceremony with their parents. This ceremony has been held yearly for over a decade. Students, caregivers, parents, and staff come dressed in their finest clothes, share an elaborate meal, and hear the prideful words of their principal and community leaders. Students receive a medallion of achievement and a t-shirt with every honor student's name emblazoned on it. Teachers write a personal comment about every child for the banquet book, which is ceremonially presented to each student. Photographs capture the event, thus creating a memory trace of the accomplishments that graces many refrigerators in local homes. In a community facing great challenges, the honor roll dinner is a powerful message of hope, accomplishment, and pride.

Like many schools, Audubon Elementary has a yearly art auction, but the auction is also a time to recognize achievements of other sorts. There is a printed brochure that describes the auction but also lists the accomplishments, awards, and grants received by staff and students for the past year. This brochure is an artifact and symbol of the triumphs and hard work of school members.

Homecomings are for alumni, who gather to tell stories of hard work and success. Returning graduates show a connection to the past and proof that their hard work has paid off. In a high school located in a low-income area, adults who have regular jobs return to remind students of the possibility of economic success. In another school, returning graduates offer to mentor struggling students and return to the school some of what the school gave them.

Special ceremonies mark the beginning or end of unique events. Transitions are important times in the lives of people and of schools. They mark the beginnings and endings of unique temporal and social events. Transitions need to be marked. They cannot go unnoticed or their importance and meaning are lost. Successful cultures find ways to highlight transitions to reinforce and build cultural values. One school celebrates the end of a planning year with a brief talk about accomplishments and challenges, followed by the awarding of pens and coffee cups to the members of the planning committee. Increasingly, schools are holding reading "challenges" to encourage summer reading. Principals mark reaching the goals in many bizarre but symbolic ways. Some have been known to eat fried worms, kiss hairy pigs, or spend the day on the roof to celebrate the school reaching its reading goals. Adding an exclamation mark to the end of special events or activities can buoy spirits and bolster values.

Memorial ceremonies are times to remember the contributions and trials of others. Most strong cultures remember those who went before. It is a way to recognize the contributions of others and connect to the history of one's school. Some schools bring back retired teachers who developed core curricular approaches or developed the special approach taken in the school. Other schools remember those who faced tragedy. At East High School in Madison, Wisconsin, students and staff place flowers on a fence where several students were killed by a reckless driver. Other schools have named scholarships or awards for student leaders who died tragically in war or in the line of duty in their professions. In a Wisconsin school, a scholarship is given each year in honor of an Irish teacher who died of cancer at a young age. The award certificate is wrapped in green and khaki—just like the green and khaki that appeared in some item of clothing the teacher wore almost every day of his career.

Elements of Successful Ceremonies

Each ceremony, tradition, or ritual works effectively if it communicates deeper values and purposes, is well organized and run, and has a touch of grandeur and specialness. Successful ceremonies often combine a meaningful set of elements (Trice and Beyer, 1985; Deal and Peterson, 1994; Deal and Key, 1998).

Special elements in ceremonies can include the following:

A special and value-linked purpose

Symbolic clothing and adornments

Symbols, signs, banners, or flags

Stories of history, accomplishment, unusual effort

A distinctive manner of speaking or presentation

An invocation of deeper purpose and values

Attention to who is invited and where they sit

Recognition of those who have shown exemplary commitment

Appropriately chosen and varied music

A carefully selected, attractive setting

Quality food or drink

Value-filled language and commentary

Meaningful symbols and artifacts

Ritual acts and ongoing traditions

The recounting of myths, legends, or stories about the school

Successful ceremonies are carefully designed and arranged to communicate values, celebrate core accomplishments, and build a tight sense of community.

Traditions

Traditions are significant events that have a special history and meaning and that occur year in and year out. Traditions are part of the history; they reinvigorate the culture and symbolize it to insiders and outsiders alike. They take on the mantel of history, carrying meaning on their shoulders. When people have traditions that they value and appreciate, it gives them a foundation to weather challenges, difficulties, and change.

There are numerous types of traditions in schools, including

Traditions that build professionalism. It is important to nourish professionalism and effort for one's students. This can happen in many ways, for example by holding retreats where energetic, collaborative planning occurs, by holding professional conferences at the school that spotlight innovative teaching by existing staff, or by acknowledging professional accomplishments in words or displays.

Celebratory gatherings where the community recognizes in story, songs, or awards the special and significant contributions of others. At one school, staff hold a storytelling contest; staff members recount stories of success or humor that occurred that year. Awards for the best story are highly sought after. When Fran Vandiver was principal of Coral Springs Middle School in Florida, many faculty meetings began with the presentation of coffee mugs to staff who had made some special attempt to serve students. Strong cultures hold a variety of ceremonies to mark special occasions, continue meaningful traditions to reinforce values, and perpetuate rituals that provide connection.

Rituals, Traditions, and Ceremonies: Two Cases

School leaders develop rituals, traditions, and ceremonies that fit with their staff and communities. The following examples show how a group of principals working with staff reinforced culture. (The first is adapted from Deal and Peterson, 1990.)

Case 1: Hank Cotton, Cherry Creek High School

Hank Cotton was principal of Cherry Creek High School in the 1970s and 1980s. The school was a large, public, secondary school located in an affluent Denver suburb. The students came from well-educated and advantaged backgrounds and were generally high-achievers; over 80 percent went on to college.

Cotton made extensive use of ceremonies, rituals, traditions, and symbols to reinforce some new priorities when he became principal. One was the behavior at graduation. At Cotton's first graduation at Cherry Creek, students threw cans, tossed paper airplanes, and were generally inattentive. Cotton told the seniors the next year that the graduation ceremony was a problem and that it needed to be revamped. He involved them in reshaping graduation to elevate its importance. Students and staff met extensively to redesign the graduation ceremony to make it meaningful and serious. Students started wearing caps and gowns in a more formal atmosphere. The ceremony became a valued occasion for students and parents.

Cotton gradually increased the number of ceremonies that celebrated academic and extracurricular success. These ceremonies were made more formal and structured and were carefully orchestrated to denote the importance of the event. Although he routinely dressed in a coat and tie, Cotton deliberately changed his "uniform" for these ceremonies. He brought a dark suit to school to change into for honors assemblies or evening award ceremonies.

As the school achieved new successes, Cotton related each to the belief in Cherry Creek's "tradition of excellence." Bumper stickers were printed stating simply, "Let the tradition continue!" and

"The Legend Lives On!" He referred to success as part of a "tradition," stating, "We traditionally send many seniors East" or "Our football team is traditionally one of the best in the state." Speaking of routine behavior as "traditional" signaled to others that these were part of a valued pattern—desirable and even inevitable.

The principal used overt school symbols with commitment and pride. An avid jogger, he would not run without the school's "bruin" on his exercise shoes. He had a set of lapel pins depicting the bruin logo of the school and wore one regularly on his sport coat. In the school, the Cherry Creek bruin is still displayed all around the buildings, on the athletic fields, and in administrative offices. Bumper stickers "advertising" the school or individual activities (the state championship tennis team, for example) are on cars throughout the district.

When the district developed a poster, "Onward to Excellence," Cotton made a mock poster for the school that read, "Beyond Excellence to Greatness," which he displayed in his office. The prevalence of these symbols and the pride with which they are worn cement the bonds among school members and communicate school spirit.

Case 2: Integrated, Yearlong Traditions

Bob Herring is principal of the Nativity School in Cincinnati, Ohio. The school is urban and serves a diverse clientele from kindergarten through eighth grade. The principal, along with his staff and the community, keep the seventy-five-year history alive and well by filling the year with ritual and tradition. The beginning and the end of the year have significant, linked ceremonies filled with history and meaning. Interspersed throughout the year, the school connects through smaller, focused traditions.

The beginning of this religiously based school starts before the first day of school. Herring gathers the new eighth graders before school to plan the opening ceremony—one that is deeply tied to the mission of the school. A procession with banners heralding the values of the school starts it. Students deliver readings and reflections

on the coming year. All new staff are introduced, from administrators through custodians; they are given a bouquet of flowers and
introduced to the community. A band made up of students, alumni,
and friends of the school plays music and provides background to
the festivities. All new students are asked to come forward—from
thirty-five-inch kindergartners to upper-level students—to receive
from one of the eighth graders a ceremonial carnation and school
button recognizing their membership in the school. The principal
recounts some of the school's seventy-five-year history, tells about
leaders and graduates who have been exemplars, and invites everyone present to become partners with the school in its quest for
learning and the right life. The ceremony ends with an environ-
mentally safe balloon launch representing, as the principal says,
"We're here, we're open, and we're ready to go!"

The school ends the year with a matching, reinforcing ceremony. Again, the band of students, alumni, and friends plays for the
assembled standing-room-only group. Tall, colorful, festive banners
signal the core purpose and values of the school. Staff who are leaving are called forward individually for flowers, thanks, and applause.
Their contributions are noted and cheered. Prayers of thanks are
given to all those who have touched the lives of the students. Staff
and parents are thanked for their support and love. The principal
and staff look back on the year, recounting stories of caring, of challenges overcome, and of accomplishments achieved. A gospel story
is read, reminding students not to hide their talents under a bushel
basket. Graduates then talk of what it means to them and how they
will use their talents for good and let their light shine in the world.
A call to the new eighth graders is given; they are to be leaders and
keep the values alive. A procession outside takes participants to a
final balloon launch—a symbolic freeing of the hopes, possibilities,
and spirit of the new graduates.

Throughout the year rituals and traditions fortify the core values of the school. On Founders' Day the histories of the early principals and teachers are retold in stories and song. Alumni return to

narrate their own memories of Nativity. The school song, written in the 1930s by a student, is sung and pondered. Every monthly faculty meeting is ended by a "Good News Report"—a ritual sharing of positive accomplishments. School assemblies become times for fun and consideration of what everyone is doing to serve each other and the values they uphold. The final faculty meeting is filled with awards for staff: for perseverance through difficult times, for implementing a new tradition, for serving an especially needy student. Each staff member has a story told of his or her contributions that year. These events throughout the year are concluded by a major ceremony in the spring.

The Nativity School leaders make rituals and traditions an important feature of their community. They build commitment and reinforce core values throughout the year while buttressing the culture by powerful ceremonies at the beginning and end of the school term.

———————

Rituals, traditions, and ceremonies make the routines of schools symbolize what is important, valued, and significant. They provide everyone a chance to reflect on what is important, to connect as a community. These are renewing and enriching parts of a school's life. But key cultural values are also reinforced and extended by the school's history and stories, which we will turn to in the next chapter.

5

History and Stories
The Importance of Symbolic Lore

Objects in the mirror are closer than they appear.

At opposite ends of the United States, two school districts reached a similar conclusion: strong roots nourish cultural cohesion and focus. As songwriter Jim Steinman notes: "Objects in the mirror are closer than they appear." This contains great truth: the past *is* closer to us than it seems to be. It affects us more than we think. The past not only shapes the present; it outlines the future. As we look backward at the past, we see that it remains embedded in existing culture.

In 1991, the West Palm Beach School District launched the new school year with a nostalgic trip down memory lane. Rather then being regaled with formal rules, several hundred administrators learned informally about the roots of the culture in their school. They were assigned to groups based on the decade they joined the district: 1960s, 1970s, 1980s, or 1990s. They were given an hour and a half to sort through the events of their decade to pinpoint that generation's legacy to the district's traditions. As the groups started to work, the entire 1960s contingent walked out. The reason: during that turbulent decade, the district experienced a teacher walk-out; a few scars remain.

After lunch, each group presented the essence of their decade— their contribution to the district's culture. For an hour and a half, the district's heritage was recounted through raps, skits, songs, and poems. Old-timers reconnected with old memories; newcomers learned for the first time how things came to be. Everyone experienced a common bond in the pageant of history— the district's cultural roots. As the event ended, Joan Knowal, the superintendent, laid out her vision for the coming year—a new beginning grafted onto solid stock.

Several years ago in Beaverton, Oregon, a similar scenario played out. Administrators assembled for the district's kick-off event, assuming that it would unfold as usual: an outside speaker, a few team-building exercises, and a speech by the superintendent. Instead, they were loaded on yellow school buses and transported to a local winery. As they walked off the bus, they saw tables labeled by decades. People assembled around the table that represented the year they joined the district. Scribes, preassigned to the table, passed out relevant artifacts—pictures, newspaper articles, school annuals. Each group prepared a presentation for the larger gathering. From early beginnings to current realities, the history was recounted through drawings, poems, songs, and dramatizations. The decade-by-decade accumulation of traditions and ways was now shared by everyone. As the sun set behind the historic building, administrators reboarded the buses and returned home. The next day, the superintendent laid out his hopes and dreams for the coming year, connecting his vision to learnings and lessons from the past.

Cultural Roots

Past events influence present cultural practices in dramatic fashion. Knowing the history is critical to a deep understanding of the culture of a school. One of the first things a physician or psychotherapist does is to review a patient's history. That's the only way to make an accurate diagnosis of a current condition. Likewise, leaders need to initiate, one way or another, an in-depth and comprehensive history of their school. Most often, it is wise to make this a public event rather than a private undertaking. A school principal in New

York State, for example, turned over half a day of the new year's staff development event to veteran teachers. Their job: recount the school's fifteen-year heritage. After the successful event, the principal observed: "It had a profound impact on newcomers, but an even stronger impact on the old-timers. I guess the only thing worse than not hearing about the past is knowing the history without anyone to tell it to."

Cultural Assessment

Cultural patterns and traditions evolve over time. They are initiated as the school is founded and thereafter shaped by critical incidents, forged through controversy and conflict, and crystallized through triumph and tragedy. Culture takes form as, over time, people cope with problems, stumble onto routines and rituals, and create traditions and ceremonies to reinforce underlying values and beliefs.

What are the forces that nudge a culture in one direction or another? Formal and informal leaders articulate direction and purpose through their words and deeds; crises and controversies forge new values and norms in the crucible of tension and strife. People, through their everyday activities, spin out unstated rules governing relationships and conflict. Planned change, while not often highly successful, leaves its traces and mementoes. Cycles of birth, death, and renewal leave a rich sediment of secrets and sentiment.

How Schools Deal with History

Like individuals, schools have varied responses to the past. Some, like the West Palm and Beaverton examples, celebrate history in public festivals. Others have negative histories, and staff still harbor anger that past events played out as they did. The scars are there but are left to fester, infecting the present with a pessimistic, negative tone. There is widespread fear that problems of the past will repeat themselves in hurtful ways.

Still other schools suffer from historical amnesia. People refuse to acknowledge and honor the past, believing that only the present and future are important to educational attainment. They are in organizational denial.

Our view is that, in large measure, past is prologue. A learning organization is one that mines past and present experiences for important lessons and principles. Through trial and error people learn what works and what doesn't. Across time, triumphs and tragedy accumulate in cultural codes—a legacy of shared wisdom that lets people know what is the best or right thing to do. Recounting history transmits these important precepts, giving meaning to cultural practices and ways.

Without roots an organization wanders aimlessly, often repeating past mistakes and failing to learn from success. As an example, a Broward County, Florida, principal was describing a past year's disaster. She was trying to instill in teachers a sense of empowerment—they could take charge and make decisions on their own. She arranged for a consultant from a local bank to offer a day-long session on empowerment. In the midst of the session, teachers revolted and asked the consultant to leave. His message wasn't seen as relevant or of much help. The principal was devastated and vowed never again to try to empower the school's teachers. As her story ended, an observer said, "Wait a minute. Didn't that event demonstrate that teachers could take charge? In trashing the empowerment session, teachers empowered themselves. What a great lesson—as long as it is made explicit. You thought you failed. In fact, you were a resounding success. Why not write the history that way?"

How does the history of the school affect the culture of today? As we noted in the definition, the elements and character of organizational culture are initiated at inception, shaped over critical incidents, forged by controversy and conflict, and crystallized by use and reinforcement (Schein, 1985; Deal and Kennedy, 1982). The culture becomes what it is over time as people cope with problems, establish routines and rituals, and develop traditions and ceremonies that strengthen and sustain the underlying norms, values, and beliefs. Over time the informal crystallizes into shared norms and values. Over time the core assumptions become norms that cannot be broken.

A school leader can get an initial reading of a school by asking a few key questions, such as the following, about the founding, traditions, and past key events of the school:

How long has the school existed?

Why was it built, and who were the first inhabitants?

Who has had a major influence on the school's direction? What were core values?

What critical incidents occurred in the past, and how were they resolved, if at all?

What were the preceding principals, teachers, and students like?

What was the school's architecture supposed to convey?

Additional elements of history should also be investigated to understand the culture. Questions on the following topics offer further guides to the examination of a school's history:

Leadership. Formal and informal leaders help provide direction— a sense of purpose and mission. Who were the formal and informal leaders of the school? What did they stand for? What new approaches, structures, or ideas did they bring to the school? If the school is relatively new, who were the founding principal and teacher-leaders?

Crises and controversies. Crises, controversies, or conflicts forge norms and values of the culture by hardening assumptions in the crucible of strife. What were the major crises, controversies, or conflicts that staff had to face over time? What was the source of the difficulty? How did staff resolve the conflicts? Did they go underground and hold the anger for years? Did they address the differences directly and honestly? Did part of the staff leave on account of the disagreements? Was some accommodation or compromise reached to rebuild a sense of community? Are the issues still part of an ongoing set of concerns and negative memories?

People, personalities, and relationships. The individuals and personalities of people who inhabited an epoch in the school's history establish ways of interacting with others. They form the unstated rules for relationships and interaction. Who were the people who made the school what it is? What were they like? How did they treat others in the building? What kinds of relationships developed over time and became the way of treating people, staff, students, and parents?

Birth, death, and renewal. All schools face waves of birth, death, and renewal among people, values, and programs. How these critical borders are traversed will affect future transitions. How were new programs, approaches, or instructional philosophies initiated, implemented, and, at times, ended? How was the sadness of losing a staff member (through firing, death, or retirement) dealt with? What were the incidents of renewal as the school took on exciting and successful new programs, people, or plans?

Changes, modifications, and adjustments. Change is never easy. The aftermath of positive and negative memories stays on, sometimes for decades, in memories. The ways the school dealt with changes in program or people, modifications of goals or educational philosophies, and adjustments of schedules and methodologies are often remembered. They can surface whenever new changes begin.

What have been the changes in curriculum, in instruction, and in the use of time and materials? How have new technologies been introduced and used? How have changes in the types, needs, and ethnicity of students in the school been greeted? How have shifts in the goals, outcomes, or standards been embraced by staff, students, and community?

How schools face their history. Like people, schools have varied responses to their history and the critical incidents that make up their shared past. Often, staff reactions to the past parallel the reactions to death and dying (Kübler-Ross, 1969). Some staff feel anger that the past events occurred. Others are in denial, refusing to acknowledge that anything happened. Some experience fear; they worry that the problems of the past may materialize again.

But some educators use history to learn for the future. Those who have dealt with history directly often feel internalized acceptance, power, and control. They know that they have learned from previous experience and can cope with anything life throws at them. They have transformed negative experiences into personal centeredness.

Successful schools nourish the heritage that brought them to the present. In doing so they reconfirm Burton Clark's (1972) observations of the reason unique colleges succeed. These organizations relied on a saga or historical narrative to unite faculty, students, administrators, staff, and alumni into a "beloved institution." That is also possible in elementary and secondary schools.

Stories

History is an aggregate of stories about people and events sorted in terms of their epic character. Historical narratives stand the test of time. But like all organizations, each school day produces dramatic events that become stories; through telling and through use, these "little stories" carry values and convey morals. Sometimes they provide comic relief; other times they offer poignant testimony to core values and deep beliefs. Too often, these important tales have a short lifespan and die shortly after the event occurs because no one sees their cultural significance. Every school generates stories each day that tickle the fancy, warm the heart, and say a lot about what school really means. Here is an example.

An elementary principal in Louisiana had a particularly rough day. She was a new principal in a tough situation—a rural school with a history of problems. At day's end, she discovered that two female students, kept after school by their teachers, had missed the bus. In a rural setting this poses a problem because the only alternative transportation is provided by parents, who were informed of the situation. The father arrived in his truck. He was a little man with a big temper. The principal first saw this as a real opportunity to establish her authority and do some P.R. but changed her mind as the father screamed in her face. "Where's the principal, I want to give her a piece of my mind." The principal smiled and replied calmly, "I'm sorry, she's not here right now."

This story is funny, but it also reinforces the values of creativity and humor. All administrators have been in similar situations. Stories allow them to appreciate the common predicaments that everyone shares and to chuckle about what they convey about life as a school leader.

But other stories are more poignant and moving, providing a glimpse into a school's significance in the life of students. Here are two examples:

In a Texas school, a student had never won an award before. But he qualified for a faithful-attendance award. His attendance was not perfect but still exemplary. Just before the award ceremony, the student was diagnosed with cancer. All he could talk about was how much he wanted to receive his "prize." Tragically, two days before the event he passed away. The school invited the parents to receive the award posthumously on behalf of their son.

A group of leaders from schools in North Dakota were invited to share stories about their work. After a lengthy silence, an older woman stood up and said, "I'm not a school leader, I'm a parent. But I want to tell you about my son. He was a very poor student, not real motivated, periodically in trouble. He turned in an assignment to one of his junior high school teachers. She turned it back, telling him he could do better. It made a difference. The next year, Mr. Ames, a biology teacher, did the same thing but also invited my son to take a biology field trip. Later my son graduated from college and is now a high school biology teacher. I thank all of you. You really can make a difference."

Schools are filled with poignant stories of teachers who made a difference, students who turned around, and tough situations that were transformed into joyful events. When these stories become part of the shared lore, they come to life and reinforce cultural commitments and values. It's not always the literal details of a story that generate power. It's the figurative interpretation that carries the rich meaning of what school is really all about.

Telling stories that exemplify the importance and quality of collegiality can reinforce successful cultures. When school principals and teachers recount positive stories of the school to students, to parents, and to newly hired staff, it communicates what is important and expected. Stories of times when staff worked together on projects or when they shared ideas, materials, and support reinforce positive cultural values.

During hiring interviews and initial visits, potential staff members are listening closely to learn what the school values and how it works. This is a key time to tell stories of hard work, collaboration, and service to all students.

Staff new to a school are in a heightened sense of awareness as they join the group and try to read the culture. It is an important time to tell stories that exemplify what the school stands for, what is valued, and what has been accomplished. These stories should be real, engaging, and richly textured to capture the imagination of the listener. Stories are powerful ways of communicating values, reinforcing norms, and celebrating cultural accomplishments. Principals and other school leaders tell stories of many different types and for very different purposes.

Hank Cotton, the principal of Cherry Creek High School who was introduced in Chapter Four, provides a good example. Cotton and his staff often reinforced norms of performance and success by recounting stories of the school's achievements. Their stories communicated what was important in a simple and direct way. They helped bind his faculty to the school by making them feel part of a successful, lively, interesting, and select organization. Cotton was a veritable library of stories of the success of individuals who exemplified the values and traditions of Cherry Creek High School. In talking with outsiders, newcomers, or media people, he would start the conversation with a set of stories of successes at the school. His staff often retold them.

The themes of Cotton's dozen stories were (1) the importance of innovation, (2) the need for hard, continuous work to achieve success, (3) the ways that quiet students or teachers finally achieve success through continuous struggle, (4) the ways teachers work together to improve classes and enjoy each others' company, (5) the importance of recruiting and selecting only the best teachers available, (6) the importance of varied, quality cocurricular activities to provide choices that meet the needs of students, and (7) the ability of teachers to make a difference in the lives of students. The stories Cotton told covered the range of values, beliefs, and assumptions that expressed the values undergirding the emerging culture.

The Cultural Network

When it comes to history or stories, those in formal leadership positions have a lot of informal helpers. Every school has its network of informal players whose important responsibilities never appear in an organization chart or in job descriptions (Deal and Kennedy, 1982; Deal and Peterson, 1990). Their scope of work unfolds behind the scenes, sometimes underground. The mix of these roles varies from school to school but most often includes priest and priestesses, storytellers, gossips, and heroines.

Priests and priestesses are the "keepers of the values." They are guardians of cultural values and beliefs, letting neophytes know how people work in the school and the history of traditions. In one restructuring school, the priestess made sure that new hires were told about the history of change and the prior efforts of staff, and also learned the core values of the school. In another school the priest was also the storyteller; he was given the podium at the yearly art show to recount the accomplishments of the year just past and to remind the school of how far they had come.

Storytellers are powerful and indispensable members of the cultural network. Storytellers furnish the school with a willing and engaging source of knowledge and lore about the school that energizes, bonds, and inspires the culture. Most people remember and respond to stories of success and accomplishment more than they do to quantitative descriptions. Although numerical depictions are useful, the crisp, personal story provides a vivid representation of what has transpired. Storytellers are often assisted in their efforts at preserving and perpetuating the school lore by the unofficial grapevine.

Gossips thrive in every organization because they provide the real-time information and scuttlebutt that everyone wants to know about. They have insider information on decisions, changes, staffing, and personnel that is usually not supplied in memos and open meetings.

Forget about e-mail; make sure that the gossips for all the major informal networks are given information early and accurately. They will get it out to everyone on their network. In one school the school council made sure that the gossips for both the resistant staff and worried parents were filled in whenever a key decision was being considered. This got out quickly to their networks, reducing the carping and griping about being "in the dark."

Spies are the secret observers of what is going on; they pass intelligence information to open ears. Every time key school leaders attend conferences or seminars, spies quickly acquire data on the topics, interests, and opinions of participants. Spies keep people rapidly informed but can also solidify resistance. "Positive" spies want to know that new ideas and programs are possible; they motivate the active staff member. "Negative" spies are simply seeking current information on intentions in order to squelch or blockade the effort. For example, in one school, staff regularly attended a voluntary leadership retreat to talk about the coming year and goals for the school. A group of social studies teachers who did not want change in any form would find out at the end of each day from a spy what was being discussed so they could find education articles to counter the ideas.

Finally, heroes and heroines persevere in every culture. To be a hero or heroine, one doesn't have to be Joan of Arc, Martin Luther King, Jr., or Patton. One only needs to be an exemplar of the core values of the culture. In one school the hero was the custodian of twenty-five years who always arrived early, always had a kind word for people, and every summer painted two rooms in the school so that by the end of his time, he had painted the entire school twice. In another school the heroine was a counselor who helped distressed children with care and attention but offered support and advice to staff as well. She was always professional, from the first day she came to work in the school to the last day. Heroines and heroes show us what we can become. They provide the culture with an image of the best that is in us.

The informal cultural network is a crucial component of a school. Leaders nurture and support the positive players of the network. Specifically, school leaders should know who resides in the central roles of the network; consult priests or priestesses at critical junctures, especially before launching major changes; provide stages for storytellers; anoint heroes and heroines whenever possible; use gossips to pass information; and reinforce, nurture, and support the network.

Historical lore and contemporary stories form the anchor and spirit of school culture. Principals, as historians and storytellers themselves or relying heavily on the informal network, can add depth and zest to a school. Everyone—students, teachers, staff, administrators, and parents—can share past exploits and current drama. In the sharing they create bonds that last a lifetime and connect with the real meaning of education. The deeper meanings in the culture also flow through the symbols and signs of people and places—cultural elements we will turn to next.

6

Architecture and Artifacts
The Potency of Symbols and Signs

As the principal assumed her new post, she remembered the promise she had made to herself during the interview to *get rid of Mr. Meany*. Mr. Meany, the middle school mascot, resembled a cross between a warlike gremlin and a grumbling troll—a rather terrifying creature. To her and others on staff, the mascot represented precisely the opposite of what she wanted the school to be— a warm, nurturing, and peaceful place. She bided her time until the Thanksgiving break. On Friday, with the help of other allies on the staff, she removed the large figure from the school's foyer and took Mr. Meany to the basement. Once school resumed, she felt quite pleased with herself. No one mentioned Mr. Meany's absence. She assumed he wasn't missed and started to think about how the school would come up with a new mascot—one that was more in tune with the cultural values she had in mind.

Between Thanksgiving and Christmas, however, there was an unusual amount of buzzing and whispering in hallways and in the teachers' lounge. Whenever she approached such gatherings, the conversations abruptly ended. Something was wrong, but she couldn't put her finger on what it was. Over Christmas she asked the custodian to come to her office. She asked him if he had any idea what was amiss. He came right to the point: "You kidnaped Mr. Meany and buried him in the basement. Mrs. Smith rescued him and now has him hanging on the wall of her classroom." The new principal and her supporters received their first lesson in the role symbols play in school culture.

What Are Symbols?

Symbols represent intangible cultural values and beliefs. They are the outward manifestation of those things we cannot comprehend on a rational level. They are expressions of shared sentiments and sacred commitment. Symbols infuse an organization with meaning, and they influence behavior. Anyone who doubts the power of symbols in our modern world should review the controversy around "Joe Camel," the animal caricature the R. J. Reynolds tobacco company used in their advertisements for Camel cigarettes. Joe Camel was viewed by parents and the public as a prime factor in encouraging teenage smoking. One of the stipulations included in a proposed settlement with U.S. tobacco companies was that the use of Joe Camel, or any other animal likeness, in advertising be prohibited.

Symbols are cultural rallying points. They represent those intangible values that are difficult to express. Architectural forms convey values, as do the symbols and signs that adorn walls. And leaders are living logos; through their words and deeds they signal what's really important.

The Power of Symbols

Symbols, as representatives of what we stand for and wish for, play a powerful role in cultural cohesion and pride. Attachment to shared symbols unifies a group and gives it direction and purpose. As our new principal quickly discovered, removing cherished symbols, irrespective of their potential negativity, carries great risk. Tampering with signals of importance is like playing with fire. In designing buildings, creating displays, naming schools, or choosing logos, we must be mindful of the signals being sent. Symbols play a more prominent role in schools than many initially suspect.

What is often labeled as fluff is more often the stuff of leadership and culture.

Symbols and Signs

Schools have a panoply of symbols and signs scattered throughout classrooms, hallways, and gathering places. This rich mix of symbolic artifacts either makes schools meaningful sanctuaries for students and celebrations of accomplishment, or dead and empty vessels of bureaucratic control. Some of the more obvious symbolic artifacts include the following:

Mission statements. In Joyce Elementary School, messages and symbols of purpose and mission are displayed everywhere. Enlarged for easy visibility, the mission statement hangs in the main hallway. Posters exhorting students to greater achievement adorn classrooms and gymnasiums. Teachers wear school pins to communicate their beliefs in students. In another elementary school, the school pin worn by teachers is in the form of a frog. It represents the transformation of frogs to princesses and princes; the school embraces that transformation as its core purpose.

Displays of student work. Good schools usually festoon the halls with displays of the hard work of students. Examples of student work are evident everywhere in good schools. The hallways are galleries symbolizing student creativity and accomplishment.

Banners. Banners exhorting students to work hard, do well, let their intelligence shine through, and excel are hanging in the halls of many schools. At Nativity, they also are carried proudly during the opening and closing ceremonies. These bright, colorful symbols help everyone remember the deeper purposes of diligent effort in the service of learning.

Displays of past achievements. In Ganado Primary, student work is displayed everywhere. In addition, awards the school has received (of which there are many) are prominently exhibited. T-shirts and book bags from different early childhood conferences are arrayed chronologically along with the awards. Superbly crafted rugs donated by local weavers decorate the walls.

Symbols of diversity. In a Wisconsin elementary school, the creativity of new immigrants is merged with the value of their new home. The walls are adorned with intricate and beautiful Hmong stitchery in which images of an American eagle are created. In another school, the flags of every nation represented in the community are raised each morning in front of the school. The cultural diversity of the Madison Memorial High School in Madison, Wisconsin, is represented prominently in life-sized plaster sculptures of teenagers from many ethnic and racial backgrounds. The display stands prominently and proudly as a symbol of shared community.

Awards, trophies, and plaques. Athletic awards, trophies, and records of the season's scores in various sports are traditional representations of the value of athletic competition. But more and more schools are recognizing, with equal relish, the academic and artistic successes of students and staff. In many schools now, beautiful display cases accommodate trophies, plaques, and academic honors of the school, and these are larger and more prominent than the sports trophy case.

Halls of Honor. Audubon Elementary School houses a "Hall of Honor" where every award received by a student or teacher is matted and framed. Newspaper articles featuring the school or a staff member are added to the mix when they appear. Copies of published articles, interviews, or poetry written or published by staff or students are also on display. The hallway is a powerful and visible testimony to the hard work and accomplishment of individuals and teams within the school (Deal and Peterson, 1996).

Mascots. We opened the chapter with an example that shows how deeply mascots fit into people's emotions and their ideas about what things mean. School mascots are tangible symbols that represent intangible values; they are the spirit that welds a school into an organic whole.

Historical artifacts and collections. The history and traditions of a school are important symbols of longevity and sustained purpose. Schools with no clear sense of history are disconnected from the past; they are rootless and lack meaning. As a counterexample, one school displays textbooks of bygone eras (from McGuffey readers to current tradebooks), the tools of writing from the past (from Esterbrook fountain pens to BIC ballpoint pens to retired computer screens), and the photos of groups of children from years past. The display reinforces a shared embrace of roots and historical progress.

Symbolism of the Physical Plant and Architecture

The physical environment and architecture of schools communicate meaning. Students and staff spend much of their time in a school building. Children, in fact, spend more than fourteen thousand hours there over twelve years of schooling. The physical setting and the school's symbolic appearance have a lot of time to exert an influence. As Cutler (1989) points out, the architecture of schools reflects important beliefs as to what schools are about and the meaning they hold for students and for the community. In the late nineteenth century, schools were often fashioned after factories, communicating a working atmosphere of efficiency and production. Later, many schools were designed to look like castles. They had towers, limestone decorations, dark oak stairways, and monumental paintings in the halls. More recently, architects have worked closely with educators and have designed schools that communicate a more personal, intimate learning environment. These trends in architectural design reflect an evolution in the way we think about education.

The symbolism of architecture reinforces culture in four major ways:

Architecture signals what is important. A school that has a small library or gigantic gymnasium sends a clear message of priorities. In some schools the largest and most luxurious sections are the athletic facilities. At Ganado Primary, visited in an earlier chapter, the library is large, airy, and in the middle of the school. It conveys the central importance of reading, learning, and success.

Architectural elements of schools can tie a community together. Where the designs, colors, and other elements used in the building connect to a community's ethnic or cultural heritage, it tightens the bonds between the school and its community. In one New Mexico Pueblo, for example, a school principal fought a successful battle with a superior over whether the school's perimeter would be enclosed by a metal chain-link fence or encircled by an adobe wall in the architectural tradition of the Pueblo. Her stance was dictated by her strong belief that the school should reflect community values (Martinez, 1989).

Architecture provides a message of deeper purposes and values. The size, grandeur, complexity, and spatial arrangements of a building communicate significant messages about what's important and what really matters.

Architecture motivates staff, students, and community by forging pride in their school. If it is dilapidated, dirty, or poorly landscaped, it becomes an eyesore rather than a symbol of pride. The tall sculpture outside in the front of Ganado Primary School that we described earlier represents a holy place to the Navajo people. It also symbolizes the knowledge students receive and is a key source of school pride.

Even the physical appearance of the school grounds sends a message. At Joyce Elementary School in Detroit, the small yard in front is carefully manicured by the joint efforts of staff, students, and community. The small patch of grass and flowers represents the care and attention students receive and is a pleasant oasis in a neighborhood that is otherwise dotted with boarded-up homes.

Schools built by the Cuningham Group in Minneapolis and other architectural firms are reflecting the architect's understanding of the power of symbols; these firms have focused on making architecture a visible symbol of a school's underlying values and purposes while providing spaces that are beautiful and functional.

School Names as Signals and Signs

Even though not all schools are named for an actual person or place (large urban areas often provide only numbers, for example, PS 142), many names provide clues to both students and community about the school's meaning and cultural values. The significance of some names has been lost to historical neglect, losing a prime opportunity to build cohesion and identity. In contrast, the John Muir School in Madison, Wisconsin, bestows symbolic power with its name. Each year features a John Muir week when the values of the famous environmentalist are highlighted and recognized. These commemorations tie students and teachers to values the school holds most dear.

Living Logos

What is a living logo? Principals and other leaders convey powerful symbolic messages as they go about their daily routines. They transmit meaning and values in all the seemingly mundane things they do. Leaders, both formal and informal, convey important messages and meanings in their words, actions, and nonverbal announcements. Their worklives are placards, posters, and banners of symbolic meaning.

This symbolic signaling occurs through the things they read, words they use, issues they raise, ideas they float, and the things they get upset, exuberant, or frustrated about. Other indicators are the educational books they buy, read, and talk about, the workshops and conferences they attend, the things they notice and discuss when visiting a classroom, and the things they write about. Types of symbolism conveyed by the actions of leaders include the following:

The symbolism of action. How principals spend their time sends a powerful symbolic message. John Flores, a strong instructional leader at Visitacion Valley Middle School in San Francisco, talks to dozens of students while taking a visitor on a tour of classrooms. Barbara Karvelis spends time on the playground at Edison Elementary School in San Francisco connecting with students, talking with parents, and leading the Pledge of Allegiance, even though she has administrative reports to finish. What leaders pay attention to sends a strong message of core values.

The symbolism of the school tour. School leaders send strong messages as they tour the school, talk to students, share ideas with teachers, and visit classrooms. They connect to the organizational core of schools—the classroom—and make time to interact with students and staff.

The symbolism of intellectual engagement. Charles Baker reads history and philosophy as well as the most current educational books. He constantly talks about the ideas he finds.

The symbolism of writing. Sigmund Boloz writes poetry about teaching, learning, and schools. He writes letters to students who have written him to make use of the school post office.

The symbolism of communicating ideas. Debbie Meier (1995) speaks eloquently about new ideas in secondary education and keeps a journal of issues and dilemmas. Her memos to staff, students, and parents are profound discussions of issues in the school, from school violence to trust, from instruction to assessment.

The symbolism of advocacy. Phyllis Crawford is an articulate and continuous advocate for her school, pressing the central office and the local community to support innovative staffing and approaches that serve students. She can describe the core values of the school to any age group and does so at every possible opportunity.

The symbolism of collegial sharing. Teacher-leaders in Audubon Elementary discuss the best innovative workshops while preparing their daily materials for class. In other schools, staff meet in the morning over coffee to share instructional ideas or seek help on problems.

The symbolism of warm greetings. A staff member is a living logo at an elementary school in San Francisco as she greets non-English-speaking parents with a big smile, words of greeting in their own language, and a cup of coffee.

The symbolism of song. At Nativity School, the original song written in the 1930s by a student still inspires and motivates. In another urban school, staff and students each month select a popular song that communicates hope and self-respect, as well as the potential in everyone. The lyrics are reprinted and used as part of a reading program; the message is discussed to build self-esteem and motivation.

The symbolism of joy, laughter, and fun. At Visitacion Valley Middle School in San Francisco, administrators, teachers, and aides are often smiling, laughing at student jokes, and approaching situations with humor. They send messages of joy rather than epistles of incarceration. In other schools, administrators and staff share the funny stories found in all schools to get through hard times and remember the humanity of teaching.

The symbolism of storytelling. In one school the teacher-storyteller recounts the history and events of the school to all visitors to the building. Similarly, at Ganado Primary, student tour guides in vests escort guests around their school while proudly recounting the school's history and successes.

The symbolism of recognition. Administrators and staff leaders wear the school colors, fasten badges proclaiming the chess club regional winners, or talk about the successes of the school to communicate their pride in achievement and effort.

The symbolism of professional learning. Staff who cannot wait to hear national speakers or one of their own staff talk about educational reform, new curriculum possibilities, and innovative instructional techniques send and model the value of learning new ideas, growing professionally, and seeking new ways to serve students. In some schools it is a badge of honor to be the teacher chosen to share a new technique.

Educators, students, and community connect in powerful ways to the symbols and logos of a school. They identify with these mundane but inexpressible signs of their institution with emotions and sentiments that last a lifetime. School leaders need to think twice about their school's artifacts, architecture, symbols, and signs. In their daily contacts and communications, they also need to be aware of what their deeds and actions say to others. Symbols, signs, and signals link everyone to the deeper purposes and meaning of the school.

In the following chapter, we see how school leaders pull these elements together to build different but powerful cultures.

7

Putting It Together
Three Schools

Knitting the elements of culture into an artistic tapestry is like creating a word from the letters of the alphabet. Juxtaposed with one another the letters form a meaningful expression, just as combining the elements of culture create a cohesive school identity. In this chapter, we explore how three principals, working with other leaders, formed a strong school culture from symbolic elements: purpose and values, ritual and ceremony, history and stories, architecture and artifacts. Because each set of challenges is different, each cultural profile is unique. But the general principles and lessons to be learned are the same.

Charles Baker, Wheaton Warrenville South High School

Charles Baker is the principal of Wheaton Warrenville South High School—a large, public secondary school located in a middle-class suburb west of Chicago. The school serves students from two different communities: students from well-educated and affluent homes as well as students from blue-collar families. A relatively new school (built in 1993), Wheaton Warrenville South replaced Wheaton Central, which had served the two communities for almost a century. The way Baker handled the closing of a venerable old institution and the move to a renovated building provides a good example of how a leader makes extensive use of ceremonies, rituals, traditions, and symbols to reinforce important values and beliefs (Vydra, 1998).

Wheaton Central High School was closed when it became obvious that the renovation it needed was too expensive to be considered. The closing of a high school is never easy, but Baker portrayed the move as one a family that had outgrown its house and needed a larger one would make. He worked with students to determine what artifacts should be taken from the old school and moved to the new home. At the final graduation at the old school, Baker distributed personal notes he had written on orange cardstock (school colors are orange and black) to the four hundred graduating seniors. The notes asked that the students join him at graduation in singing a special song. There was not a dry eye in the house as the seniors joined Baker in singing "Auld Lang Syne," a fitting tribute and closure to the end of an era.

Baker helped students make certain that Wheaton Central traditions became part of the new way of doing things at Wheaton Warrenville South. After the move, the students helped decide the best ways to incorporate the old school's seal and motto: "Scholarship, Commitment, Tradition, and Integrity." At the old school each of the four main hallways had been named for one of the words engraved on the school seal. This created a problem in the new school; there were only three hallways. Students solved the problem by suggesting that the hallways should be named for the first three values because Integrity should be part of the school's foundation.

When the school board pushed Baker and the students to accept new colors and start over with new traditions, symbols, and icons, students refused to budge. With Baker's support they insisted that only the Tigers, the motto "Sempre Tigris," and the colors orange and black could continue the proud traditions and heritage of their school. Nothing else could or would do.

Students and faculty sorted through more than one hundred years of Wheaton Central memorabilia to determine what artifacts should be displayed in the new Tradition Hall. Among the most treasured items now on display are those donated by the widow of the "Galloping Ghost," Wheaton's football hero, Red Grange. Students had kept in close touch with Grange's widow until her death.

School history now comes to life in a walk through Tradition Hall. School tradition remains alive through the Principal's Pin, which is a duplicate of the old school seal and is given by Baker to students who distinguish themselves at the school, community, district, state, or national level.

Through storytelling, Baker underscores the importance of ritual, history, traditions, and celebrations. Once each year at the homecoming assembly, Baker brings out a new chapter in the story of "Tom the Tiger" and reads it to the enthralled students. Two years ago the story related how Tom called on his old friends, the Blues Brothers, to help him defeat the homecoming opponents and crown the homecoming queen. As the story goes, Tom the Tiger got to know the Blues Brothers through John Belushi, himself a Wheaton graduate. Adding drama, a local pair of actors who regularly perform at Chicago Bulls basketball games joined Baker at the microphone. The Blues Brothers' antics and music had all of the school's students and teachers revved up and dancing in the aisles. Although Baker is the one who writes and reads the latest exploits of Tom the Tiger, he also has played other dramatic roles at pep assemblies. One year he dressed in tiger garb complete with a tiger head and orange tights. In costume, he danced down the bleachers to the song "Bad to the Bone." The students rose to a fever pitch when he took off the tiger head and revealed that the dancing tiger was their much-loved principal. The very next year he brought a live tiger cub to a schoolwide homecoming assembly. As a mascot the Wheaton Warrenville South's tiger influence is widely felt. Baker's office is filled with tiger memorabilia, and his clothing is always resplendent with a tiger-paw pin, a tiger-embroidered emblem, or some form of tiger pride. "Sempre Tigris" is a motto with deep meaning. Baker wants to make certain that each graduate leaves the school knowing the Tigers are always with him or her.

A few years ago a nationally recruited senior football player came down with encephalitis during a spring vacation in Florida with his family and became gravely ill. The next fall the football team dedicated their season to the former Tiger. The entire student body paid tribute to him in an all-school assembly—a reminder to everyone that Tigers are bonded forever. The football team won the state championship that year, and his parents credit his subsequent progress to the support he received.

Baker regularly gives Tiger Paw pins (done in different colors and shapes each year) to those teachers, staff members, parents, and community members who help the high school reach its goals. A local store owner who donates supplies to the speech team or a teacher who gives dozens of hours to a committee might walk away with a Tiger Paw pin and a note of gratitude from the principal. Many faculty members proudly display years of accumulated Tiger Paws in their classrooms.

Tiger posters are auctioned off periodically to faculty members who can answer questions publicly about the school and about real Siberian tigers. Baker accomplishes two symbolic purposes with these auctions. He makes certain that all faculty members know that tigers are near extinction and encourages them to support efforts to save the species. He also gets Tiger memorabilia distributed into more of the classrooms.

Knowing that not all students are motivated by athletics, Baker uses the tiger to support other values, such as environmental responsibility. The tiger cub that appeared at the homecoming assembly has been adopted by students who raise the more than $2,000 needed for its annual care and feeding at an Arkansas refuge. The South Tigers rejoice in their adoptee's spirit and willfulness, even though the grown animal is not allowed to visit the school. Other students collect money to support tigers in the wild in India and Siberia. Still other students are involved in preserving local habitats that surround the school and have mounted a large Prairie Project that protects the natural ecology of a nearby forest preserve.

Students are continually challenged by the principal to be the best they can possibly be. A published playwright, Baker knows how to use drama to entice and enthrall. His speeches are always memorable, whether to the National Honor Society or to the volleyball team. One year he asked National Honor Society students what they would choose if stacks of *Schindler's List* videotapes or Snoop, Doggie, Dog CDs were their alternatives. He went on to challenge the students' choices by encouraging them to make a difference with their lives—to be a Schindler rather than one of the masses simply listening to popular music. Another year, Baker showed incoming freshmen the grade book for the class of 1902, which he had taken from the school archives. He recalled the story of how one of the Wheaton students from 1902 discussed her courses and her grades. Baker noted a section at the bottom of the student's report card called "deportment" and mentioned that this might be an unfamiliar word. He went on to explain why deportment was just as important in 2002 as it was in 1902. It is part of the school's cultural heritage.

Rick DuFour, Adlai E. Stevenson High School

When Rick DuFour accepted the principalship of Adlai Stevenson High School in 1983, he inherited a suburban Illinois high school with a structure and culture that reflected a traditional commitment to sorting and selecting students into watertight categories (Vydra, 1998). Incoming students were ranked from highest to lowest on their performance on a single, nationally normed test. They were then assigned to one of five ability levels on the basis of that ranking. Strict caps and quotas ensured that each incoming class was distributed among the five levels, according to a bell-shaped curve. School personnel spent a great deal of time dealing with students and parents who aspired to placement in a higher-ability group. Students who had difficulty in classes were recommended by teachers for a less rigorous level. As a result, hundreds of downward-level transfers were initiated each semester. Teachers often defined their job as presenting information clearly, assessing a student's aptitude and work ethic, and promoting academic success by placing students at the appropriate ability level.

DuFour began by engaging faculty, parents, staff, and students in extended discussions regarding the kind of school they hoped Stevenson might become. Throughout the dialogue he made a conscious effort to provide participants with the information they needed to arrive at informed decisions about future directives. He shared research on effective schools, gathered information on the academic performance of top schools in the state, compiled data on Stevenson students, and presented countless examples of how the school fared in comparison with others. Gradually, consensus emerged as to what Stevenson High School might become. A vision statement was written, endorsed by all parties, and adopted as board policy.

The vision statement provided a blueprint for the school's improvement efforts. While it provided a general direction for improvement, DuFour attempted to sharpen the focus by engaging the faculty in a series of questions. He asked the faculty to move beyond the affirmation of the belief that "all children can learn" to address such questions as, What do we expect all students to learn in each of our courses? How will we respond to students who do not initially achieve the intended learning? How can we provide these students with more time and support for their learning? What collective commitments must each of us make to ensure that all our students learn? What criteria do we use in assessing students' work? What are our strategies for improving upon the results we are getting?

As the faculty discussed these questions, discrepancies between the school they envisioned and the actual conditions at Stevenson became more apparent. Structural changes were initiated to assign students to courses on the basis of proficiencies rather than quotas. Remedial programs that perpetuated low performance were eliminated, and support systems were put in place to provide additional time and assistance for students in need of help. Grading systems were modified to provide students with more timely feedback. Courses that had been reserved for the select few were opened to all. Task forces were created to address specific areas of the school's operation and to identify strategies for improvement. Teacher-leaders became active participants in the cultural transformation.

Although these structural changes presented significant challenges, shaping the culture of the school to support its new direction was a far more complex undertaking. Beliefs, expectations, and assumptions that had previously guided the school were no longer appropriate, now that it was committed to finding new ways to help all students meet high academic standards. Now the school hired only teachers who had a clear sense of what they were trying to accomplish, who connected their purpose with the experiences and interests of their students, and who motivated and inspired students to believe in themselves and their ability to be successful in school. Above all else, a school truly committed to every student's success needed teachers who were willing to accept responsibility for students' learning.

At every faculty meeting DuFour began to relate stories of teachers or instructional teams who were reaching above and beyond the call of duty to help students achieve high academic standards. He shared stories about, for example, a social studies teacher who suggested that sophomores be admitted to an Advanced Placement course and who then went to extraordinary lengths to ensure that all of the students qualified for college credit by earning a high score on the College Board exam. He told stories of teachers in the math, English, science, and social studies departments who developed an experimental two-year interdisciplinary program and what they had learned as a result of their efforts. He told the story of the English department's effort to eliminate remedial courses by developing a writing center to assist students who experienced difficulty in their classes. He told the story of a teacher who went to the home of a student to confront him about his absences from school. As he told each story, he presented the teacher being recognized with a small plaque—

a "Super Pat," for Super Patriot (the school's nickname). Initially teachers were uncomfortable with public recognition of individuals because it was a departure from a more acceptable general praise: "You are the best faculty in the state—everyone is equal."

DuFour emphasized that the school had to identify and celebrate examples of commitment to its vision statement. He invited all staff members to nominate colleagues for Super Pats and share their stories of extraordinary efforts. Gradually teachers began to come forward with nominations and became informal leaders of the celebrations. Part of every faculty meeting was devoted to the presentation of Super Pats. In the eight years of DuFour's principalship, over five hundred Super Pats were presented to members of the Stevenson staff.

Stories of collective achievement became another standard feature of Stevenson's faculty meetings under DuFour's leadership. He searched constantly for evidence of improvement—in grade distributions, reduced failure rates, improved attendance, higher levels of student or parent satisfaction. He looked for gains on standardized achievement tests, increases in the number of students exceeding state standards on state tests, reductions in suspensions, and so on. With the passage of time his reports to the faculty offered more longitudinal data, comparisons, and trends to demonstrate that the collective efforts of the staff were making an important difference.

Parents and students acted as additional sources for stories that paid tribute to staff members. At every meeting of parents, he asked parents to notify him whenever a teacher went to great lengths to help a student achieve academic success. Each year he surveyed seniors to identify the teachers who had the greatest impact on their lives. Then four times each year he published excerpts from these parent and student tributes in an internal "Kudos Memorandum" to remind teachers of the significant impact they were having and to offer living examples of commitment to student learning.

Celebrations and traditions were also used to shape the Stevenson culture. Each school year began with a "Happy New Year Party" that was planned and orchestrated by the faculty leaders. Accomplishments and milestones (weddings, births, graduate degrees, and special times) of staff members were publicly acknowledged and applauded. New staff were introduced, presented with their official staff t-shirts, and then led in a recitation of a humorous "faculty pledge." Orientation time was devoted to a review of the school's history, vision, and priorities rather than administrative trivia. The board of education hosted a back-to-school dinner dance for all staff to extend their wishes for a great school year. A "Quarter Century Club" was established to honor those who had served the school district for twenty-five years, and longevity pins were presented to staff for every five years of service. The school hosted an annual formal dinner party for teachers appointed to tenure. A part of the senior awards program was devoted to honoring teachers who had earned some form of external recognition or were among those cited most frequently by seniors as having had a positive impact on their lives. An annual appreciation luncheon was inaugurated to honor staff members who had volunteered their time to work on school improvement task forces or to serve as a mentor to a new colleague. Special ceremonies were created to pay tribute to retiring staff members.

So, what was the result of these efforts? In the year prior to DuFour's arrival, the local community had defeated a badly needed referendum, a major section of the community had started a petition drive to annex itself to another district, and the state had refused to forward the school's application for the United States Department of Education's (USDE) Excellence in Education Award. During the eight years of DuFour's tenure the community passed two referenda. Stevenson became the first in the county to receive the USDE award and the first in the state to receive the award a second time. Although DuFour left the principalship in 1991 to become superintendent of the Stevenson district, the stories, Super Pats, Kudos Memoranda, celebrations, and traditions have continued under the leadership of many people. Since 1991 Stevenson has been cited as one of America's best high schools on five occasions by national magazines and has become one of ten schools in the nation to receive the USDE award for a third time.

Joan Vydra, Hawthorne Elementary School

Joan Vydra became principal of Hawthorne School at the same time the school boundaries changed, and it welcomed an increase of low-income students (Vydra, 1998). This was the first time in its almost forty-year existence that it was faced with a diverse clientele. The clash of cultures loomed close on the horizon: neighborhood families with conservative values and the "bus" students who were perceived to have value systems that didn't fit the neighborhood standard. Vydra had to move fast to establish common rituals and traditions that would bring different groups together in a cohesive culture and celebrate success for *all* students. Throughout her first year she worked with parents and staff to examine whether older, established ways would benefit all students.

Influenced by the work of Nel Noddings, she felt that a culture of care was essential to student success. At the end of her first year, a parent wrote a note expressing her thanks for all that was done by "the little school with the big heart." Vydra seized that theme as the centerpiece of Hawthorne's culture.

Care Week became the school's fall tradition. During the first day of Care Week, students learned how important it was to care for themselves. On Tuesdays, students showed they cared for their families by writing thank-you notes to their parents. On Wednesdays, classrooms were celebrated as students figured out ways they could show they cared for each other. On this day each student had his or her picture taken with the classroom teacher, who wrote a personal note to each student. Thursday found the students cleaning up and caring for the school. On Friday the focus went more global, as each year the students decided on a different charity to support—a local food pantry, homeless shelters, or an orphanage. In the spring the school worked with parents to create an all-school planting day. Each student brought a plant to school (or received one at school) and went outside at a predetermined time to plant the annuals or perennials in new flowerbeds surrounding the school. Different families then signed up to care for the flowerbeds throughout the summer. Hawthorne students who used to regularly trudge through the landscaping became protectors of the grounds because they had helped to plant and care for them. Caring was becoming a way of life at Hawthorne.

Within two years the school had successfully given parent volunteers a role far beyond that of the traditional room parent who baked for parties and went on field trips. Every classroom had a head liaison parent who worked with other parent volunteers. Parents took on many different roles. For example, parent publishers helped publish student writing and parent sunshine providers organized meals when families experienced tragedies. Additionally, the principal and staff worked with several families to "adopt" other families in which parents had never felt any personal success in school. These were the disenfranchised who typically did not support school, who did not bring their children to programs or to parties, and who seemed not to care.

The school reinforced the value of student success by ensuring that every decision made by faculty and parents was predicated on its contribution to student accomplishments in the classroom or in life. Teachers learned to make plans and purchases as steps in the road to improved achievement. The principal worked with teachers and parents to make certain they shared the vision of success for every student every day. When the first-year review revealed that new arrivals were the only students who did not achieve standards, Vydra used the results to celebrate the school's overall success while simultaneously calling attention to what needed to be done to make certain new students were given whatever resources necessary for success.

Parents received a newsletter every week that featured current events and calendar activities as well as things parents could do to improve achievement, to build self-esteem, and to contribute to the school's success. The school routinely included stories of student and classroom success and achievement in the newsletter. The principal used the newsletter to explain to parents that the "Hawthorne Way" of doing things was similar to the Golden Rule. This was something regularly stressed with students at each assembly, as they boarded the buses, or got ready to walk home each day. These efforts started to bear fruit. When a substitute teacher began to tell second-grade students about the behavior she expected to see at an assembly later that afternoon, she was interrupted by a student who told her that students would never misbehave at an assembly because "that was not the Hawthorne way of doing things."

Vydra promised the teaching staff that she would do whatever she could to make sure there was nowhere in the world teachers would rather teach than at Hawthorne. She shared her fervent belief that there was no greater calling than teaching and worked hard to put the best teachers into Hawthorne's classrooms. She made certain that school culture was an important part of the interview process each time a team looked for a new teacher. Applicants were prepared with questions such as, What is one nonnegotiable value for your classroom? Who is one of your curriculum heroes and why? How do your students know you care about them each and every day? How would you describe the school and classroom in which you most want to teach?

The interview team understood that Hawthorne wanted teachers who would not only be great in the classroom but also great for Hawthorne—teachers who understood the importance of unifying events that build a strong school culture.

Teacher-leadership was widespread. Every Hawthorne teacher chaired at least one all-school event and served on at least two other committees. Committees planned events like Care Week, Literacy Week, Earth Week, Family Math Night, Family Sciences Night, Curriculum Night, Field Day, All-School Song Fest, and the Year-End Celebration. All events were planned to bring the entire school community together in ways that enhanced the curriculum,

helped parents become partners in the learning process, or celebrated student success and achievement.

Teachers worked together easily. They learned to appreciate different gifts that each of them brought to the table. The principal
encouraged staff to visit other teachers' classrooms. At one faculty
meeting teachers were surprised that in lieu of a regular agenda, they
had a treasure hunt to find a specified list of items. Teams searched
every nook and cranny of the school to find the special and unique
things that each teacher had done within his or her room. On
another occasion, teachers were given a week's notice that they
were not to plan any instruction for a Thursday afternoon. The
teachers returned from an all-school field trip that morning, during
which they had seen *The Wizard of Oz* performed at a local high
school. Upon their return, each teacher found a bag of straw, a
notepad of hearts, and a roll of tinfoil in the classroom. These were
the props with which they were to plan with their students and then
carry out the afternoon's lesson. The creative ritual was formally discussed at the next faculty meeting and then informally celebrated
for weeks to come.

Celebrations and play were a very regular part of Hawthorne. Faculty meetings became times of celebration of teacher success, as stories were shared and teachers recognized. At other meetings
risk-taking teachers were frequently acknowledged by having candy
tossed their way. Vydra used playful ways to celebrate the hard work of
teachers. For instance, when teachers completed student progress
reports they found a pack of Extra gum in their mailboxes to thank
them for the extra time they had to spend completing the task. On
another occasion teachers found Lifesavers in their mailboxes with a
note thanking them for all the lifesaving work they did for students
day in and day out. Snickers bars were the reward when there was
something that it would be better to laugh at than to cry about.
Teachers were given squirt guns on a hot spring day and bubbles on
another occasion. End-of-year celebrations were especially memorable. By the end of her fifth year at Hawthorne, Vydra had convinced

100 percent of the teachers, office staff, and instructional aides to entertain the students. Slides celebrated the accomplishments of students throughout the year with songs sung by each grade level, providing a year's walk down memory lane. The culminating event was a compendium of skits and songs performed by the staff members. Parents and students grew to love and look forward to this closing ritual. Leadership transformed the culture of Hawthorne.

Three Schools, Three Cultures

Three schools, three different challenges, three unique cases of cultural and academic success—each principal focused on the elements of culture that made the most sense, given the situation. Baker and his staff capitalized on tradition, stories, and a mascot that reinforce school spirit. DuFour and his informal leaders emphasized developing a shared belief that all students can succeed and on stories, recognition rituals for teachers, and all-school ceremonies of various types. Vydra and her staff brought a divided community together by emphasizing the values of caring and universal success, as well as by telling stories and using playful rituals and ceremonies.

In addition to showing how the elements of culture can be knit together to enhance or improve life in schools, these three principals exemplify the virtues of symbolic leadership. The different roles symbolic leaders play that were described in this chapter will be the focus of the next.

Part II

The Leadership Challenge

Eight Roles of Symbolic Leaders

As we have already established, culture arises in response to persisting conditions, novel changes, challenging losses, and enduring ambiguous or paradoxical puzzles. People create culture; thereafter it shapes them. But we have also shown that school leaders can nudge the process along through their actions, conversations, decisions, and public pronouncements.

Effective school leaders are always alert to the deeper issues agitating beneath a seemingly rational veneer of activity. They read between the lines to decipher complex cultural codes and struggle to figure out what's really going on. Once they get a bead on a situation, they ponder over whether and how to try to shape or reshape existing realities. In effect, they are asking three basic questions: (1) What is the culture of the school now—its history, values, traditions, assumptions, and ways? (2) What can I do to strengthen aspects of the culture that already fit my idea of an ideal school? and (3) What can be done to change or reshape the culture, when I see a need for a new direction?

As they labor to meld past, present, and future into a coherent cultural tapestry, school leaders assume several symbolic roles in their work to shape features of the culture.

Reading the Current School Culture

How do school leaders read and shape the cultures of their respective schools? To find that out, we borrow from anthropology and coin our own metaphors for school leaders' roles: historian, anthropological sleuth, visionary, symbol, potter, poet, actor, and healer.

It is important to remember the formidable nature of school leaders' unofficial power to reshape school culture toward an "ethos of excellence" and make quality an authentic part of the daily routine of school life. As we mentioned earlier, school leaders must understand their school—its patterns, the purposes they serve, and how they came to be. Changing something that is not well understood is a surefire recipe for stress and ultimate failure. A leader must inquire below the surface of what is happening to formulate a deeper explanation of what is really going on. To be effective, school leaders must read and understand their school and community culture.

Reading culture takes several forms: watching, sensing, listening, interpreting, using all of one's senses, and even employing intuition when necessary.

First, the leader must listen to the echoes of school history as we noted in Chapter Five. The past exists in the cultural present.

Second, the leader should look at the present. Most important, the leader must listen for the deeper dreams and hopes the school community holds for the future. Every school is a repository of unconscious sentiments and expectations that carry the code of the collective dream—the high ground to which they aspire. This represents emerging energy that leaders can tap and a deep belief system to which he or she can appeal when articulating what the school might become.

A school leader can get an initial reading of the current culture by posing several key questions about the current realities and future dreams of the school (Deal and Peterson, 1990):

What does the school's architecture convey? How is space arranged and used? What subcultures exist inside and outside the school? Who are the recognized (and unrecognized) heroes and villains of the school? What do people say (and think) when asked what the school stands for? What events are assigned special importance? How is conflict typically defined? How is it handled? What are the key ceremonies and stories of the school? What do people wish for? Are there patterns to their individual dreams?

Shaping a School Culture: The Roles of School Leaders

When school leaders have reflected and feel they understand a school's culture, they can evaluate the need to shape or reinforce it. Valuable aspects of the school's existing culture can be reinforced, problematic ones revitalized, and toxic ones given strong antidotes.

Everyone should be a leader. The eight major leadership roles to be listed next can be taken on by principals, teachers, staff members, parents, and community leaders. Cultural leaders reinforce the underlying norms, values, and beliefs. They support the central mission and purpose of the school. They create and sustain motivation and commitment through rites and rituals. It is not only the formal leadership of the principal that sustains and continuously reshapes culture but the leadership of everyone. Deep, shared leadership builds strong and cohesive cultures.

School leaders take on eight major symbolic roles:

Historian: seeks to understand the social and normative past of the school

Anthropological sleuth: analyzes and probes for the current set of norms, values, and beliefs that define the current culture

Visionary: works with other leaders and the community to define a deeply value-focused picture of the future for the school; has a constantly evolving vision

Symbol: affirms values through dress, behavior, attention, routines

Potter: shapes and is shaped by the school's heroes, rituals, traditions, ceremonies, symbols; brings in staff who share core values

Poet: uses language to reinforce values and sustains the school's best image of itself

Actor: improvises in the school's inevitable dramas, comedies, and tragedies

Healer: oversees transitions and change in the life of the school; heals the wounds of conflict and loss

School Leaders as Historians

As noted earlier, effective school leaders probe deeply into time, work, social, and normative events that have given texture to the culture of a school. They realize that echoes of past crises, challenges, and successes reverberate in the present. Leaders perpetuate an understanding of where the school has been as a key factor in interpreting present practices and ways. Staff and parents take on this role whenever new people arrive or new parents join the community.

One of the best ways of tracking the past is to construct an "organizational timeline" that depicts the flow of events, ideas, and key personages over several decades. This provides a chronological portrait of the events, circumstances, and key leaders who shaped the personality of the school.

School Leaders as Anthropological Sleuths

Anthropological sleuths are just what the name depicts—a cross between Margaret Mead and Columbo—serious students of the culture as well as dogged detectives. Both roles are important, as school leaders listen and look for clues and signs to the school's present rituals and values.

School leaders must unearth the pottery shards and secret ceremonies of daily activity in teachers' lounges, workrooms, and hallway greetings that reflect deeper features of the culture. Nothing is ever as it seems, and one must look for unexpected interpretations of common human activity.

For example, in one innovative school teachers started wearing the drug program badge that states, "Just Say No." They did it, not to reinforce drug awareness week but to uphold their desire to slow the pace of curricular change for a little while. Knowing the meaning of the badge was important to understanding the culture.

School Leaders as Visionaries

In addition to their role as historian or anthropologist, school leaders must also be visionaries. Through a careful probe of past and present, they need to identify a clear sense of what the school can become, a picture of a positive future. Visionary leaders continually identify and communicate the hopes and dreams of the school, thus refocusing and refining the school's purpose and mission. To arrive at a shared vision, they listen closely for the cherished dreams that staff and community hold. They probe for the latent sentiments, values, and expectations for the future and bring these to the front for public discussion, consideration, and enactment.

Developing a shared vision for the school can motivate students, staff, and community alike. It is not simply for the leader; it is for the common good. By seeking the more profound hopes of all stakeholders, school leaders can weave independent ideas into a collective vision (Deal and Peterson, 1994).

Visionaries can be found anywhere in a school. For example, in Chicago's Piccolo Elementary School the president of the local school council, who was a parent and community leader, joined with the principal to identify and communicate the hopes and dreams for the school. Together they worked to focus on developing a caring, safe, and academically focused learning environment. Another example: At Hollibrook Elementary, the principal and the teachers jointly shared and protected the vision for the school, even as staff and administration changed. When Suzanne Still, the principal, and some teachers left for other positions, remaining staff leaders helped preserve the dream by pulling the new principal into the collective vision.

School Leaders as Symbols

Everyone watches leaders in a school. Everything they do gets people's attention. Educational philosophy, teaching reputation, demeanor, communication style, and other characteristics are important signals that will be read by members of the culture in a variety of ways. Who school leaders are—what they do, attend to, or seem to appreciate—is constantly watched by students, teachers, parents, and members of the community. Their interests and actions send powerful messages. They signal the values they hold. Above all else, leaders are cultural "teachers" in the best sense of the word.

Actions of leaders communicate meaning, value, and focus. We rarely "see" an action's symbolic value at the time it occurs. More often we realize it later, as it soaks in. For example, the principal's morning "building tour" may be a functional walk to investigate potential trouble spots or building maintenance problems. In some schools, teachers and students see the same walk as a symbolic event, a ritual demonstrating that the principal cares about the learning environment. Similarly, the visit of a teacher-leader to another's class to observe a unique and successful lesson can send the message that instruction is valued.

Schools are filled with many routine tasks that often take on added significance. Routine tasks take on symbolic meaning when leaders show sincere personal concern for core values and purposes while carrying them out. A classroom visit, building tour, or staff meeting may be nothing more than routine activity—or it can become a symbolic expression of the deeper values the leader holds for the school.

Almost all actions of school leaders can have symbolic content when a school community understands the actions' relevance to shared values. Seemingly innocuous actions send signals as to what leaders value. This is done in many ways, but five possibilities are as follows:

Symbolize core values in the way offices and classrooms are arranged. A principal's office, for example, sends strong messages.

Its location, accessibility, decoration, and arrangement reflect the principal's values. One principal works from her couch in an office in the school's entryway; another is hidden in a corner suite behind a watchful and protective secretary. One principal decorates her office walls with students' work; another displays athletic trophies, public service awards, posters of favorite works of art, and photographs of his family. These social artifacts signal to others what the principal sees as important.

The arrangement of classrooms also sends a powerful message. Is student work displayed? Is it current? Is there a wide variety of learning activities, materials, and books readily available? Do teachers have a professional library, awards, or certificates for professional institutes nearby? Physical arrangements reverberate with values.

Model values through the leader's demeanor and actions. What car a leader drives, his or her clothes, posture, gestures, facial expression, sense of humor, and personal idiosyncrasies send signals of formality or informality, approachability or distance, concern or lack of concern. A wink following a reprimand can have as much effect on a child as the verbal reprimand itself. A frown, a smile, a grimace, or a blank stare—each may send a potent message. Do staff interact with students and parents when they cross into school territory? Are energy and joy apparent in the faces of teachers?

Use time, a key scarce resource, to communicate what is important, what should be attended to. How leaders spend their time and where they focus attention sends strong signals about what they value. A community quickly discerns discrepancies between espoused values and true values by what issues receive time and attention. The appointment book and daily routines signal what a principal values. And whether staff attend and engage in discussions with parents during Parent Association Meetings or site-based council gatherings shows what the culture holds most dear.

Realize that what is appreciated, recognized, and honored signals the key values of what is admirable and achievable. School leaders signal appreciation formally through official celebrations and public recognition and rewards. Informally, their daily behavior and demeanor communicate their preference about quality teaching, correct behavior, and desired cultural traditions. Staff and students are particularly attentive to the values displayed and rewarded by various school leaders in moments of social or organizational crisis.

Recognize that official correspondence is a visible measure of values and reinforces the importance of what is being disseminated. The form, emphasis, and volume of memos and newsletters communicate as strongly as what is written. Memos may be a source of inspiration, a celebration of success, or a collection of bureaucratic jargon, rules, and regulations. Class or departmental newsletters can send a message to parents that communication and connection are important. Even the appearance of written material will be noticed, from the informality of the penciled note to the care evidenced by the new color inkjet printer. Pride, humor, affection, and even fatigue displayed in writing send signals as to what a school's leaders value.

Taken together, all these aspects of a leader's behavior form a public persona that carries symbolic meaning. They come with the territory of being a school leader and play a powerful role in shaping the culture of a school.

School Leaders as Potters

School leaders shape the elements of school culture (its values, ceremonies, and symbols), much the way a potter shapes clay— patiently, with skill, and with an emerging idea of what the pot will eventually look like. As potters, school leaders shape the culture in a variety of ways. Four illustrations of how leaders shape school culture follow:

They infuse shared values and beliefs into every aspect of the culture. It often falls to the principal, formally and informally, to articulate the philosophical principles that embody what the school stands for. A valuable service is rendered if the principal and other leaders can express those values in a form that makes them memorable, easily grasped, and engaging. But teachers are also powerful communicators of values whenever they meet parents in the hallway, run into a school board member in the grocery store, or jog with a local businesswoman. What they say and do sends messages about the school and its values as compellingly as if they were giving a speech.

Values are often condensed into slogans or mottos that help communicate the character of a school. Of course, to ring true they must reflect the school's practices and beliefs. Examples are (1) "Every child a promise" (2) "A commitment to People. We care. A commitment to Excellence. We dare. A commitment to Partnership. We share" and (3) "A Community of Learners" (Deal and Peterson, 1990). In some schools, symbols take the place of slogans but play a similarly expressive role. As noted earlier, one middle school's values are embodied in the symbol of a frog. The frog reflects the school's commitment to caring and affection that eventually can turn all children into "princes and princesses."

They celebrate heroes and heroines, anointing and recognizing the best role models in the school. There are important individuals in most schools, past and present, who exemplify shared virtue. Heroes and heroines, living and dead, personify values and serve as role models for others. Students, teachers, parents, and custodians may qualify for special status and recognition through words or deeds that reflect what a school holds most dear. Like stories about Amelia Earhart or Charles Lindbergh, the stories of these local heroes help motivate people and teach cultural ways. When heroes exemplify qualities a school wants to reinforce, leaders can recognize these individuals publicly. Schools can commemorate teachers or administrators in pictures, plaques, or special ceremonies just as businesses, hospitals, or military units do.

They observe rituals as a means of building and maintaining esprit de corps. School leaders shape culture by encouraging rituals that celebrate important values. As noted earlier, everyday tasks take on added significance when they symbolize something special. School activities may become rituals when they express values and bind people in a common experience.

These rituals are stylized, communal behavior that reinforces collective values and beliefs. Here is an example:

> A new superintendent of schools opened his first districtwide convocation by lighting a small lamp, which he labeled the "lamp of learning." After the event, no one mentioned the lamp. The next year, prior to the convocation, several people inquired: "You are going to light the lamp of learning again, aren't you?" The lighting of the lamp had been accepted as a symbolically meaningful ritual.

Rituals take various forms (Deal and Peterson, 1990). Some rituals are social and others center around work. Americans shake hands, Italians hug, and French people kiss both cheeks when greeting or parting. Surgical teams scrub for seven minutes, although germs are destroyed by modern germicides in thirty seconds. Members of the British artillery, when firing a cannon, still feature an individual who holds his hand in a position that once kept the horse from bolting because "that's the way it has always been done."

Meetings, parties, informal lunches, and school openings or closings provide opportunity for rituals. As we saw earlier, Herring closed meetings by offering an opportunity for anyone to share stories of positive events. In this setting, issues can be aired, accomplishments recognized, disagreements expressed, or exploits retold. These rituals bond people to each other—and connect them with deeper values that are otherwise difficult to express.

They perpetuate meaningful, value-laden traditions and ceremonies. Schoolwide ceremonies allow us to put cultural values on display, to retell important stories, and to recognize the exploits and accomplishments of important individuals. These special events tie past, present, and future together. They intensify everyone's commitment to the organization and revitalize them for challenges that lie ahead.

When an authentic ceremony is convened in a hallowed place, given a special touch, and accorded a special rhythm and flow, it builds momentum and expresses sincere emotions. Planning and staging these events is often done with extreme care. Encouraging and orchestrating such special ceremonies provide still another opportunity for leaders to shape—and to be shaped by—the culture of the school. Here is an example:

> One group of parents—with input from the high school leadership—planned a joyous celebration for the school's teachers. They decorated the cafeteria using white tablecloths and silver candle holders. They went to the superintendent and asked permission to serve wine and cheese and arranged for a piano bar where teachers and parents could sing together. Each teacher was given a corsage or a ribbon. The supper was potluck, supplied by the parents. After dinner the school choir sang. Several speakers called attention to the significance of the event. The finale came as the principal recognized the parents and asked everyone to join her in a standing ovation for the teachers. The event was moving for both the teachers and the parents and has become a part of the school's tradition.

School Leaders as Poets

We should not forget the straightforward and subtle ways that leaders communicate with language—from memos to mottoes to sagas and stories, as well as in informal conversation. Words and images invoked from the heart convey powerful sentiments. "The achievement scores of my school are above the norm" conveys a very different image from "Our school is a special temple of learning."

Acronyms can separate insiders from outsiders to the school community and tighten camaraderie. (They can also exclude people.) PSAT, CTBS, or NAEP may carry different meanings to educators than to their public. Idioms and slogans ("Every child a promise" or "We Care; We Dare; We Share") may condense shared understandings of a school's values. However, hypocrisy in such slogans can alienate those who hear them. Consider the principal in the satirical book *Up the Down Staircase* (Kaufman, 1966) who would say, "Let it be a challenge to you" in the face of problems that were obviously impossible to solve.

Metaphors may provide "picture words" that consolidate complex ideas into a single, understandable whole. Whether students and teachers think of a school as a factory or a family will have powerful implications for day-to-day behavior.

As we have seen, one of the highest forms of culture-shaping communication is the story. A well-chosen story provides a powerful image that addresses a question without compromising its complexity. Stories ground complicated ideas in concrete terms, personifying them in flesh and blood. Stories carry values and connect abstract ideas with sentiment, emotions, and events.

Stories told by or about leaders help followers know what is expected of them. They emphasize what is valued, watched, and rewarded for old-timers and greenhorns alike. For example, the parents of a third-grade student informed the principal that they were planning to move into a new house at Christmas and would therefore be changing schools. He suggested they tell the teacher themselves, since she took a strong personal interest in each of her students. They returned later with the surprising announcement that they were postponing their move. The principal asked why. The mother replied, "When we told Mrs. Onfrey about our decision she told us we couldn't transfer our child from her class. She told us that she wasn't finished with him yet."

By repeating such stories, leaders reinforce values and beliefs and so shape the culture of the school. Sagas—stories of unique accomplishment, rooted in history and held in sentiment—can convey core values to all of a school's constituents. They can define for the outside world an "intense sense of the unique" that captures imagination, engenders loyalty, and secures resources and support from outsiders.

School Leaders as Actors

Cultures are often characterized as theater, that is, the stage on which important events are acted out. If "all the world's a stage," then aspects of the life of a school are fascinating whether they are comedy, tragedy, drama, or action. Technically, they have been called "social dramas"; the various stages of activity in the school cross all forms of theater.

Much of this drama occurs during routine activities of the school. Periodic ceremonies, staged and carefully orchestrated, provide intensified yet predictable drama in any organization. In crises or in critical incidents (like the murder of students in a school yard or the explosion of the space shuttle Challenger) are moments of unforeseen school drama.

A critical incident like a school closing gives leaders a significant opportunity to act in a social drama that can reaffirm or redirect cultural values and beliefs. An example: A principal was concerned about the effect of a school merger on the students and the community. He convened a transition committee made up of teachers and community members to plan, among other things, a ceremony for the last day of school. On that day, the closing school was wrapped in a large red ribbon and filmed from a helicopter. When wreckers had demolished the building, each student, teacher, parent, and observer was given one of the bricks tied with a red ribbon and an aerial photograph of the school tied with a red bow (Deal and Peterson, 1990).

Such drama provides a heightened opportunity to make a historical transition and reaffirm cultural ties within the school community. Rather than inhibiting or stifling such dramas, school leaders may seize them as an opportunity to resolve differences and redirect the school.

Social dramas can be improvisational theater with powerful possibilities to reaffirm or alter values. In a political sense, such events as faculty or student conflicts are arenas—with referees, rounds, rules, spectators, fighters, and seconds. In the arena, conflicts are surfaced and decided rather than left lingering and seething because they have been avoided or ignored. Such avoidance often leads to the development of toxic cultures or subcultures. Critical incidents from this perspective provide school leaders with a significant opportunity to participate in a social drama that can reaffirm or redirect the values and beliefs of the school.

School Leaders as Healers

Most school cultures are stable but not static, and changes do occur. School leaders can play key roles in acknowledging these transitions—healing whatever wounds they create and helping the school adapt to change in terms of its traditions and culture. Leaders serve as healers when

They mark beginnings and endings. Schools celebrate the natural transitions of the year. Every school year has a beginning and an end. Beginnings are marked by convocations to end the summer and outline the vision and hopes for the coming year. Endings are marked by graduations, which usually unite members in a common celebration of the school culture.

They commemorate events and holidays of cultural importance. The observation of national and seasonal holidays, from Cinco de Mayo to Presidents Day, may make the school an important cultural center for events in the local community and reaffirm the school's ties to the wider culture. One school convenes a schoolwide festival each fall, winter, and spring, at which they demonstrate the way the students' religions honor a particular holiday. Because of the diversity among students, such festivals provide an opportunity for students to learn different customs and foods. Such observances create a schoolwide unity around differences that could otherwise become divisive.

They remember and recognize key transitional events in the occupational lives of staff. The beginning and end of employment are episodic transitions that a principal may use to reaffirm the school's culture and its values. What newcomers must learn about the school is a good definition of what is important in its culture. Even transfers, reductions in force, terminations, and firings-for-cause are transitions that can be marked by cultural events. In one Massachusetts elementary school, primary students named hallways after teachers who had been let go in the wake of a taxpayer rebellion that required tremendous cost reductions in nearly every school in the state (Deal and Peterson, 1990).

They deal directly and openly with critical, difficult, challenging events in the lives of staff and students, always aware of the message they are sending. Unpredictable, calamitous events in the life of the school, like a death or a school closing, will be upsetting to all members of the school community. These transitions require recognition of pain, emotional comfort, and hope. Unless transitions are acknowledged in cultural events, loss and grief will accumulate. For example, at one school following the death of several classmates by two snipers, the school and its community came together at funerals, services, and informal gatherings to remember and eulogize the students. They came together to grieve over the loss of friends, the loss of classmates, the loss of innocence. These events helped the culture cope with their pain and sadness.

School leaders as healers recognize the pain of transitions and arrange events that make the transition a collective experience. Drawing people together to mourn loss and to renew hope is a significant part of a leader's culture-shaping role. Too often, the technical side of leadership eclipses available time and willingness for its much-needed cultural aspects. As a result schools become sterile, incapable of touching the hearts of students and teachers, or securing the trust and confidence of parents and local residents. By expanding their repertoire of symbolic roles, school leaders can make a real difference. Their artistry can help galvanize a diverse group of people into a cohesive community whose members are committed to a beloved institution.

Symbolic leadership is especially needed when schools are new or when they require considerable transformation to serve their students. The unique ways schools' leaders mold culture through symbolic leadership will be explored in the next chapter.

9

Pathways to Successful Culture

Unrelenting reform, rapid change, or benign neglect can quickly undermine cultural focus and cohesion. The result: a sterile school that people tolerate because it does no harm. Neither does it do much good. Or a school can grow toxic. The result: motivation, commitment, and loyalty are destroyed across the board for students, staff, parents, and administrators. We'll have more on that in the next chapter.

How does a sterile or toxic school recapture its symbolic buoyancy and become a healthy, vibrant culture? Burton Clark (1972) has argued that new cultural forms emerge under one of three conditions: (1) when a new organization is launched, (2) when an existing organization is open to cultural evolution, or (3) when a crisis forces an organization to examine its traditional ways. In the pages that follow, we will examine four schools that exemplify one of these three pathways to building a successful culture. New York's Central Park East Secondary, launched in 1985, is an example of a school that began with a blank slate. Hollibrook Elementary in Spring Branch, Texas, and Joyce Elementary in Detroit are examples of cultural metamorphosis—schools that emerged from toxic crises to become highly successful. Dibert Elementary in New Orleans demonstrates how a school can fine-tune itself over time, evolving through the leadership of four principals into a model enterprise. Together, the four cases show three interesting pathways for cultural development or change: pioneering, overhauling, and evolving or tweaking.

Central Park East Secondary School, New York City

Central Park East Secondary School was established by Deborah Meier and others in 1985. They started the school in response to the poor performance of the local traditional high school. Meier, a former kindergarten teacher, worked to develop a new kind of school. She had a clear vision for what makes a good school: "We wanted a place where young people and their teachers could work in shared ways around topics and materials they were inclined to enjoy, for long stretches of time, and without too many preconceived structures. . . . We wanted settings in which people knew each other through each other's works, through close observation of practice" (Meier and Schwartz, 1995).

The organizers wanted a school that remained small, multiaged, intimate, and interesting; developed "strong habits of mind" in students; offered teachers "responsible control" over their professional lives; used performance-based assessments and held students to high standards; nurtured a strong professional community where discussion, dialogue, and innovation were highly valued; and promoted staff and student inquiry and investigation into pressing contemporary problems.

These original guiding principles are enacted now in everyday practice. Small classes symbolize the commitment to personalization. Time is available for staff to discuss problems, plan new curricula, and make schoolwide decisions. Passionate professionalism is bolstered through peer observations and extensive collegial feedback. During assessment, the role of "critical friend" is applied to both students and staff. Appropriate habits of mind are mirrored constantly through discussions, problem-solving retreats, and student assessments. The interweaving of these underlying beliefs and principles solidifies the culture and encourages in everyone a deep identification with the school's abiding purpose.

Leaders at Central Park East are not out of sight and out of touch. They are visible symbols of what the school values and cherishes. The way they spend their time, what they attend to, and how they direct their efforts all serve to communicate the school's values and model its principles.

Rituals and traditions in the school build on shared values. Staff would stop class in order to deal with crises, discuss challenges that arose, and deal with personal loss. The final performance assessment became a powerful tradition that reinforced the collaborative nature of learning and the high standards of the school. As new staff came on board, stories of the early days, of the development of new instructional planning, and of the constant flow of visitors reinforced emerging norms.

Meier also had the foresight to link up with the Coalition of Essential Schools, providing Central Park East with heightened legitimacy, additional resources, and external expertise. The school, which started from scratch, has shown how a positive culture can be molded in secondary education (Meier, 1995).

Hollibrook Elementary, Spring Branch, Texas

Suzanne Still, the new principal of a failing Hollibrook Elementary, did not enjoy the luxury of starting afresh—it seemed more like starting afoul. Hollibrook was considered one of the worst places for staff to work and teachers to teach. North of a major freeway and squeezed between abandoned businesses and apartment buildings in disrepair, the school was home to a mix of students from a variety of foreign countries. Ninety percent of the student body qualified for free or reduced-cost lunch programs. Eighty-five percent were Hispanic, claiming Spanish as their primary language. Students' achievement scores ranked at the bottom of the district's distribution. Parents felt disenfranchised. The school itself was in poor repair and staff morale was abysmal (Johnson, 1995; Hopfenberg, Levin, and Associates, 1993).

Like Meier at Central Park East, Still had the foresight to link up with an external program. Her choice was the Accelerated Schools Model, founded by Henry Levin, a Stanford professor (Johnson, 1995; Driver and Levin, 1997). Rather than outlining a lockstep recipe for schools to follow, the Accelerated School Program focuses attention on inner resources and potential:

A school is its own center of expertise, equity, community, risk taking, experimentation, reflection, participation, thrust, and communication.

A school focuses on the strengths it has, its inner power, vision, capabilities, and sources of solidarity.

A school has an obligation to provide all students the best education possible, to value equality of opportunity.

A school should provide equitable outcomes for students as well as equal choices for parents' participation.

A school is not a balkanized conglomerate of interest groups; it is a community.

Life experiences of students should be acknowledged and incorporated into instructional activities.

Achieving such noble ends will require a school to enhance experimentation, reflection, trust, and communication.

This flexible, philosophical base undergirded Hollibrook's new belief system and guided the school's cultural renaissance. This emergent culture supported the following ideas (Hopfenberg, Levin, and Associates, 1993; Johnson, 1995):

If the existing curriculum and instructors' techniques are not working, new ones should be found. We can find the right ones.

We should seek new ways from research, experts, or best practices.

Students learn best when instruction fits their interests and engages them as active partners.

Skills and knowledge should be integrated, not fragmented into isolated parts.

We may have our differences, but in times of crisis we pull together.

As a school we share responsibility for student learning. If students aren't learning, we have to do something about it.

Parents are our friends and colleagues, integral to our success.

We can be successful with all children.

Interaction with other professionals helps build my skills as a teacher. I can learn by talking about my craft. I want to learn.

Teaching and learning involve the whole school. As a teacher, I am valuable as a decision maker, planner, and collegial trainer.

We believe Hollibrook can become an exemplar of quality learning—for all schools.

Hollibrook's positive, emerging beliefs were reflected and reinforced in new cultural traditions such as the following (Hopfenberg, Levin, and Associates, 1993):

- Faculty meetings became hotbeds of professional discussion. Once morgue-like and dominated with administrative trivia, the weekly rituals became lush with Socratic dialogue focusing on instruction, student learning, and the deeper meaning of teaching. A common ritual during faculty meetings was a discussion of a research article selected by the principal.

- Fabulous Friday was a creative new program offering four weeks of mini-courses for students. This innovative curriculum idea provided students with a wide assortment of courses in which they could explore new content, activities, and topics.

- A parent center—"Parent University"—provided courses on parenting and other educational issues, created a heightened parental involvement, and created a strong bond of trust between parents and staff. Parents were highly valued and their contributions regularly celebrated.

- Small discussion groups were held in parents' homes through a program called "Gente a Gente." This provided an additional opportunity to break down barriers between parents and teachers.

- A shared governance council provided an arena for community problem solving and planning. As a ritual it brought everyone together around the school's premier purpose.

- Student tour guides showed the school's many visitors around the campus. They explained the Hollibrook program and radiated pride in their new shared enterprise.

Once at the bottom, Hollibrook now revels in being at the top of the class. The school is widely recognized for its excellent educational program.

Anna M. Joyce Elementary School, Detroit

Joyce Elementary demonstrates how a positive school culture can evolve over time. The school building was built in 1914 and, for a time, served as the community city hall. As the local government was absorbed into the city municipality, the building became a high school and later an elementary school. Today, Joyce Elementary sits in a largely African American neighborhood on Detroit's east side, adjacent to Indian Village—a designated historic community (Peterson and Bamburg, 1993).

Inside the school a visitor quickly senses that Joyce Elementary School is a special place. The school mission statement is enlarged to poster size and faces anyone who walks up the steps to the main office. The wide halls and high ceilings built in the early 1900s convey a feeling of spaciousness, even of grandeur.

However, it is the cleanliness, warmth, and attractiveness of the newly painted interior that commands attention. It is clear that Joyce Elementary is a loving place, carefully tended to by those who call the school home. The walls and lockers are freshly painted in bright, attractive colors. Walls and stairwells are decorated with an up-to-date graphic design. The floors are clean; there are few broken or cracked windows. The hall has display cases full of examples of student work; outstanding student performances are recognized in a variety of arenas. Lockers, running the length of the hall, are topped with carefully maintained potted plants. A designated community member carefully waters each plant. Despite its age—it's more than eighty years old—Joyce is a school obviously full of vitality and life.

The principal, Leslie Brown, Jr., has been principal for twenty years. His own demeanor, like that of the school itself, is a blending of seriousness and caring, fun and hard work. Always dressed professionally, Brown is a tall African American man with graying hair and a broad smile. For twenty years he has worked with staff and community to build a highly successful school culture.

The school's classrooms are well organized and focused on learning. While the classrooms are old, the equipment is not. A profusion of materials and equipment is available for instruction. Children are attentive to their work, and teachers engage in a multitude of instructional activities. Energy and caring are obvious everywhere. During recess and lunch the school is full of the usual chatter and fidgeting to be expected in children. Also obvious is a clear understanding about appropriate behavior, reinforced with gentle reminders from teachers.

The office is a center of activity. The school day has not begun, yet the secretary and office aides busily juggle their too-many tasks while the principal focuses on several issues that need his immediate attention. Everyone in the office is busy until the morning bell sounds. Then their attention focuses on classrooms and learning.

Joyce Elementary's growth into an exemplary school didn't occur overnight. It evolved over three periods of time. Prior to the arrival of Brown, Joyce was an urban elementary school with a traditional staff, a principal renowned for his laissez-faire leadership, classrooms that were filled with traditional methods of instruction, and few special programs. The school's metamorphosis began in 1979 with the appointment of Brown as principal.

Following his appointment, he and a new assistant principal initiated a series of key changes that laid the foundation for transforming the school. These initiatives included the formulation and articulation of a clear, student-focused mission; the initiation of a program to clean up and landscape the outside of the school; the transfer or retirement of some who did not believe in students or embrace improvement; the design of initial programs to increase involvement of parents and staff in planning school improvement efforts; and the implementation of an extensive after-school program to expand the learning and experiences of students.

These early initiatives focused attention on the needs of students, communicated that change and improvement were important, and garnered momentum for other initiatives. These early efforts were followed by a careful attention to building a school that students could feel proud to attend and come to happily, where they could become successful trying something new. Staff were sought who wanted to work toward this mission, and parents were snared to help out.

As retirements and vacancies occurred, Brown sought staff who had a commitment to change, who believed that all students could learn, and who were willing to work together for the good of the school. The culture of the school began to change slowly as new staff arrived, as parents developed renewed trust in the school, and as programs became institutionalized traditions.

The last time period in Joyce's evolution saw the school gain greater flexibility through the district's site-based decision-making program. As the school became more successful and staff more committed, there was increased interest on the part of staff and the principal to gain further independence from a highly centralized bureaucracy. Through a new program in the district, Joyce Elementary became one of Detroit's "Empowered Schools," with discretion over the budget and many of its programs.

Shared decision making evolved at Joyce. Beginning in 1990 the principal began involving parents, students, staff, and community in a school improvement planning process. In November of 1992, the staff voted (87 percent were in favor) to submit an application to be an Empowered School and thus to gain further decision-making flexibility.

As an Empowered School, Joyce gained control over its budget. It became more responsible for ensuring that resources were used to support the school's mission. This flexibility has made it possible to outfit a computer lab and place four computers in each classroom; also made possible were a local area network, an increase in staff development opportunities, improvement in the appearance of the hallways and classrooms in the school, and extensive after-school opportunities for children. By 1997 students were performing at the 75th percentile on standardized tests, fewer students were retained, attendance of both the staff and students reached 96 percent, and the school was selected as a National School of Excellence.

Core features of the Joyce culture are shared beliefs that emphasize high expectations, quality teaching, and concern for children. These features include the following:

Make student achievement and development a core mission.

Believe that all children can learn if given a chance.

Provide students with varied experiences that are fun.

Honor and recognize those who work hard and succeed.

Make the school a community center where everyone is welcome and everyone becomes a learner.

Develop independence from the district to tailor programs to serve the local clientele.

Seek out funds to increase learning opportunities.

Make the school building an enjoyable place to work in and visit.

This set of elements fosters a rich school experience, recognition and awards for effort and achievement, a deep support and belief that students can learn, a positive connection to parents and community, a proactive approach to getting things done, and an attention to purpose that keeps everyone focused on what is important and valued. Over time, school leaders developed a shared set of beliefs that are condensed in the school's mission statement.

The Joyce Elementary School Staff and Community are committed to
   . . . providing a productive learning environment
   . . . developing positive student self-esteem, and
   . . . motivating students to achieve their educational
      goals,
Thus preparing students for the future.

The school's mission statement is reflected and reinforced in other traditions and ceremonies. One element of the school's purpose is to make school a place that is fun and offers children special chances to enrich their lives. To do this the school started after-school programs in golf, tennis, softball, aerobics, drill team, Academic Games, and Future Problem Solvers.

The school also found powerful ways to bring the community together to celebrate student success. For example, the Honors Dinner, held since the early 1980s, has offered a way to celebrate students who maintain a high GPA. The dinner began with 175 attendees, including students, staff, and parents. Currently, several hundred attend. Now there are so many at the ceremony that they must televise the ceremonial event to an overflow crowd via closed-circuit television. During the occasion teachers individually let each child know what a wonderful job they have done that year and present them with a special medallion and t-shirt displaying the names of all those on the honor roll.

Another ritual is the "Clapout," an indoor parade. When something of significance happens, the staff organizes the students in the hallways, and the honorees walk through the hall to the applause of their fellow students. When 140 students posted perfect attendance during a ten-week period, the school organized a Clapout parade. Those with perfect attendance marched through the halls as all the other students clapped. Recognition, celebration, and fun characterize all cultural ceremonies at Joyce.

Parents are not simply welcomed to ceremonial occasions; they are integral participants. They have their own workshops on a variety of topics; they also help in classes and have direct involvement in decision making. Through these efforts the school has been able to actively involve parents in the education of their children, improve the quality of life at home, and help parents address some of their personal needs.

At Joyce the culture supports continuous personal and professional learning. Staff are encouraged to attend staff development workshops and seminars and to bring the ideas back to the school. Parents are provided programs for their own education. And the principal regularly seeks workshops and seminars that provide opportunities for him to learn new ideas and reflect on his leadership.

The principal's values came out when he spoke of what he thought ought to occur at a good school:

> A positive self-concept of all "stakeholders" must be promoted. Encouragement, celebration, affirmation, and

understanding should permeate the school. For example, students should have access to technology, library books, field trips, [have their] work displayed, counseling, "I caught *you* being good" awards, to name a few positive building blocks. Parents ought to feel welcome at school, volunteer, support at-home projects, prepare children for school daily, know the school's mission, policies, procedures, and calendar for maximum support. Teachers must move toward grade-level instruction, utilize technology, involve students in the design of the classroom, promote student success, involve parents and community meaningfully, and pursue staff development. The principal, the team leader, must work to keep the vision *alive*, seek and provide resources, encourage and further staff and parent development, "go the last mile," and constantly model success and positiveness.

Leslie Brown, Jr., manages the everyday complexities of the school while providing symbolic leadership that has helped the school evolve into a real treasure.

Dibert Elementary, New Orleans

One of the best examples of the growth of a school culture over time can be seen in the John Dibert Elementary School's evolution (Boyd-Dimock and Hord, 1994–1995). Over the course of many years and under the leadership of four principals, a deep and positive culture of learning, caring, and innovation has emerged.

Located on the outskirts of New Orleans in a seventy-year-old building, Dibert is a K–6 school enrolling four hundred students, the majority from low-income families. In the early 1970s Dibert was highly bureaucratic and rigidly structured, dominated by a rigid, authoritarian principal. The school subsequently recreated itself through the leadership of four principals and the school's other leaders. It became an excellent example of a "learning community" where staff feel connected to each other and together encourage creativity and productivity. The school's culture now encourages collective attention to student learning, high levels of staff collaboration, creativity, and supportive relationships through shared norms and values (Boyd-Dimock and Hord, 1994–1995).

It was not always that way. In the early 1970s, the school started losing students. At one point the New Orleans school board discussed closing the school permanently. But parents banded together to keep it open as an open-enrollment magnet school. This began the "re-creation" of Dibert.

The first principal of the new magnet school was Lucianne (Lucy) Carmichael, a creative and caring administrator, who is also a ceramic artist. She arrived with a vision. Her vision for the school included providing opportunities to develop artistic creativity, viewing the staff as the school's most important resource, and focusing on the continuous development of faculty skills and knowledge.

Under Carmichael's leadership, learning became a tradition at Dibert. The first summer, she gathered teachers for a week-long session to review the instructional program and begin to build a sense of community. Later she helped institute "Faculty Study" on Thursdays so teachers could talk about curriculum, instruction, and ways to implement a child-centered approach in classes. Staff visited other schools. Some traveled to England to visit schools implementing creative instructional approaches. Quality teaching and learning became a part of the school's values and traditions for both teachers and students.

Celebration and sharing became a central part of the way of life at Dibert. Each day the school community gathered in the basement to swap stories and to recognize student and staff accomplishments. Out of this, a real sense of family grew and flourished.

Carmichael's departure had people wondering if the same spirit would continue. Sometimes a new principal means the end of old ways. But Dibert's cultural strength survived the transition. Clif St.

Germain, the new principal, had been a guidance counselor and assistant principal. He wanted to build on the foundation Lucianne helped to foster. To the spirit of Dibert, Clif added heart, making the school a happy place where children learn and grow in an atmosphere of kindness and sharing (Boyd-Dimock and Hord, 1994–1995).

The school took advantage of the new leader's arrival to address some gnawing issues that needed attention: classroom overcrowding, more time for planning, student discipline, and building trust among staff. Time and energy were spent cleaning up and decorating the dingy facility. But extra effort was poured into ritual and ceremony. The rituals of Morning Meetings and Faculty Study continued to reinforce the values of learning and connectedness. Thursday volleyball games with staff broke down barriers. Friday gatherings at local restaurants built ties, reduced tension, and cemented trust among staff. Dibert's culture became even more personal and cohesive under Clif's leadership.

Before Clif moved on, he went to great lengths to ensure that Dibert would have a new principal who would build and reinforce the school's values and traditions. He succeeded. Nancy Picard took over as principal, believing it was her central task to continue the school's direction and focus. She added other positive touches. Through her leadership, staff sought out grants to start an Arts Connection Program. Their efforts paid off with a new arts program. Parents increased their involvement in the school through projects, time, and support. Students learned about democracy through experiences in a student council. New report cards were designed to reflect the school's values. Faculty Study was refined to focus more on professional development needs. Administrative procedures that distracted from instructional time were discontinued. Dibert's focus on professional improvement, which was deeply embedded in the culture, gained momentum.

When Picard left, the Dibert culture faced another transition. Again, it was made smoothly; the beat continued. The new principal, Wiley Ates, was as committed as his predecessors to cultural continuity and the evolution of instruction. Under his and staff leadership, the school reviewed the mission statement and core operating principles. Reflective dialogue on the curriculum fueled the energies of staff and helped address openly and honestly other issues, such as conflicts that had arisen after a strike. The continuing ritual of Morning Meetings cemented the deep bonds of students, staff, and parents. The school's symbol of the rainbow perpetuated the multicultural values of the school.

Over time the culture of Dibert Elementary School grew and strengthened. It is a culture that values learning for all; promotes a sense of togetherness and caring; supports the empowerment of staff, students, and parents; nurtures change and improvement; and provides rituals and traditions that support and illuminate the values and accomplishments of everyone.

At Dibert, school leaders built upon the previous culture, each leader adding new orientations and values.

Pathways of Successful Cultures

Each of these four schools found their way to a successful culture. The lesson here is simple and straightforward: each school will find its own path if the school has widespread leadership that can help find the right direction.

School leaders shape culture over time in a variety of ways. For example, they can

Develop a student-centered mission and purpose that motivates the heads and hearts of staff, students, and community

Strengthen elements of the existing culture that are positive and supportive of core values

Build on the established traditions and values, adding new, constructive ones to the existing combination

Recruit, hire, and socialize staff who share the values of the culture and who will add new insights or skills to the culture

Use the history (or build the history if the school is new) of the culture to fortify the core values and beliefs

Sustain core norms, values, and beliefs in everything the school does

Over time, though the individual parts may be unique, the general characteristics of positive cultures that develop are similar. Elements of positive, successful cultures are as follows:

A mission focused on student and teacher learning

A rich sense of history and purpose

Core values of collegiality, performance, and improvement that engender quality, achievement, and learning for everyone

Positive beliefs and assumptions about the potential of students and staff to learn and grow

A strong professional community that uses knowledge, experience, and research to improve practice

An informal network that fosters positive communication flow

Shared leadership that balances continuity and improvement

Rituals and ceremonies that reinforce core cultural values

Stories that celebrates successes and recognize heroines and heroes

A physical environment that symbolizes joy and pride

A widely shared sense of respect and caring for everyone

In this chapter we demonstrated how these cultural elements were woven together by the actions and reflections of school leaders who cared and who paid attention to what was important. In the next chapter we turn to the ways negativity and a lack of positive values can poison schools, creating toxic cultures.

10

Transforming Toxic Cultures

Jefferson High School (a pseudonym) is the oldest school in a California urban district. At one time, it served a population of high-achieving, wealthy students; nearly all headed for top-ranked universities or prestigious colleges. Within a relatively short period of time, the neighborhoods surrounding the high school went through a dramatic demographic metamorphosis; a majority of students after the change were low-income blacks or Hispanics. Interest in postsecondary education was low. More than a few students found a sense of connection through membership in a gang.

Rather than changing to meet the educational needs of their new clientele, teachers and administrators took refuge in the past. Negativity replaced optimism and the culture took on a strikingly negative tone. Teachers berated students and lowered expectations. Drop-out rates skyrocketed and academic performance dropped dramatically. The principal's chief function became to maintain order and keep parents at bay. Negative teachers ruled the roost. Staff regularly leaked negative information to parents and the press. A group of self-labeled "incompetent" teachers formed a "Turkey Club." Meetings held once a week after school in a local bar focused on making fun of students, plotting against the administration, and trying to recruit other colleagues into their private club. Conflict between various subfactions was handled behind the scenes, with intent to harm and undermine others. Complaining and griping in the coffee room before and after school became a widespread ritual. It was almost impossible to find a teacher with a positive attitude— or even one who would admit to having hope. To be seen as upbeat and committed to students and learning invited sure ridicule. The principal spent most periods hiding out in his office or spending time at the district building. He was a constant target of criticism and scorn. He was seen as an obstacle, and opposition to him was one of the few things that held a divided faculty together. In sum, Jefferson was a school culture in toxic free fall.

The Negative Side of School Culture

By looking at schools like Jefferson, we can learn about these negative features and discover how to change them. Many school leaders inherit a real mess and must deal directly with toxic cultures and subcultures.

Characteristics of Toxic Cultures

The following characteristics are common in toxic cultures:

They become focused on negative values. They make work better for adults, even if it takes away from students; they conduct routine, boring classes that "follow the rules"; they serve only a small group of elite students and spurn others who deserve to learn; they focus on primarily achieving outcomes that are unimportant (football championships), too low (basic skills), or undemocratic.

They become fragmented; meaning is derived from subculture membership, antistudent sentiments, or life outside work. There may be no real, positive, symbolic glue to hold people together—schools are like isolated cells or silos that people enter in the morning and leave at night. Isolated but powerful departmental or grade-level fiefdoms rule the roost. Divided along racial or ethnic lines, people organize into opposing camps. They form small cohort groups composed of those who joined the school at the same time and share similar educational philosophies. All schools have subcultures, but significant fragmentation increases friction and leads to sabotage and outright warfare. Fragmentation decreases the sense of shared mission and purpose. Staff members, like teachers, go through the motions. Little cooperation takes place. Students pick up the factionalism and take advantage of it.

They become almost exclusively destructive. Teachers talk about faculty meetings like they were Sarajevo fire-fights, with everyone "sniping" and "attacking" each other. Cabals and guerrilla groups of "negaholics" harass and attack anyone who is trying to improve the situation, develop new instructional techniques, or simply behave in a professional way. Staff and administrators dislike their clientele and generally foster negative mind-sets about students they are supposed to serve. Teachers and staff spend their energies protecting themselves, hiding out, or withholding participation.

They become spiritually fractured. In such schools there is often a lack of positive values or any sense of integrity. Most people display a sense of anomie, hopelessness, narcissism, unreflective mindlessness, or "undeadness" (a condition between being alive and being dead, as the poet e. e. cummings suggests).

In negative cultures one often finds other features that are dysfunctional or socially damaging. In these schools few positive relations exist among adults, making positive relations with students difficult. Frequently staff feel personally lost or pessimistic, discouraged, and despondent. Their sense of efficacy plummets in these schools, and the group sense of efficacy declines, prompting inaction and negativity.

Elements of Toxic Cultures

In toxic schools, the elements of culture reinforce negativity. Values and beliefs are negative. The cultural network works in opposition to anything positive. Rituals and traditions are phony, joyless, or counterproductive. The following conditions are typical:

Negative Values and Beliefs Hold Sway

Professional and certified staff champion individualism, mediocrity, and inertia. They value doing what is best for adults. They believe students "from this community" can't learn. They don't feel they can do much about it. Without core values and beliefs supporting hard work, improvement of one's craft, and attention to student learning, the educational program is placed on the back burner (if it is on the stove at all).

One toxic school was eventually "reconstituted," that is, closed and reopened with new staff and administration, because student learning was extremely poor and there was little effort to change. Negative values and beliefs suppressed what positive ideas existed. Staff openly believed they couldn't teach children who attended their school ("felt significantly inadequate"), believed it was the students' and parents' fault that students didn't learn ("blamed the victim"), and no longer searched for ways to change their instruction to achieve results ("gave up on improvement"). This was a dying, if not dead, professional culture much like the Jefferson example cited earlier.

Powerful Network Members Become Negaholics

If the most powerful members of the informal network are negaholics (Carter-Scott, 1991), pessimists, or intensely self-interested, then the messages and meanings that fill this social system will take on a negative cast. When those who are listened to fill the social space with negativism and disparaging remarks, stories, and messages, the message system becomes septic. It reinforces negativism and despair. Priests and priestesses work to undermine the efforts of new teachers or administrators. They constantly refer to the "good old days" and make sure new initiates fall victim to old ways. Gossips fill the grapevine with innuendo and the latest criticisms. Their gossip frequently moves outside the school, leaving parents to fret and attack (Carter-Scott, 1991).

Specific negative roles found in schools include

Saboteurs, who are always finding ways to sabotage, scuttle, or ruin any new idea, program, or positive activity that may occur. They know everyone's weaknesses and use them to their own advantage. Their slings and arrows are always ready, during staff meetings or planning sessions, to slay new ideas. When saboteurs are effective, they drag down enthusiasm, depress willingness to innovate, and make change nearly impossible.

Pessimistic storytellers, who remind everyone of every failure, unresolved problem, and lost opportunity that ever occurred. Or they invent horror stories of the past. Given the arena, these negative raconteurs will poison the culture and dampen energy and enthusiasm. These are not the honest individuals who remind us of problems we need to solve. Their purpose is to make us believe that the school cannot be anything but the negative, failing mess that their stories represent. Do not give them a soapbox unless they want to solve the problems they present.

"Keepers of the nightmare," who never fail to remind the staff of dreams that went awry, hopes that were dashed, and programs in the past that did not work the way they were supposed to. These negative historians reduce staff commitment by telling of the problems that developed during changes in programs or curricula.

Negaholics (Carter-Scott, 1991), who find something negative, nasty, unfavorable, or pessimistic in any ideas that are proposed. This role drags down the motivation and commitment of the group. When the negaholics dominate discussion and interaction, staff recede into their own classroom worlds and avoid working on innovative projects. Staff discussions become truncated and ineffective when negaholics are around.

Prima donnas, who want all of the best for themselves: the attention, the focus, the programs have to revolve around them. They must have center stage and the spotlight on them, even when they are not the main event. This can damage morale, dampen the sense of community, and drain energy as staff try to respond to the needy prima donna.

Space cadets, who have no idea what is going on but never try to think through what's happening. Talkative space cadets can take up important time in meetings as they ramble on about nothing. With good group process skills, they can be neutralized.

Martyrs, who expect people to see any contribution they make or time they spend as an enormous personal strain. Like the prima donnas, martyrs may have deep personal needs that they want the school to meet. They can drain energy and time if they are taken seriously.

Deadwood, *driftwood*, and *ballast*, who are along for the excursion, the glory, the excitement of teaching in a good school—and the paycheck. But they refuse to do any of the work, seldom keep up with new ideas, and never offer to assist. Deadwood are part of a department or grade level but have done little that is new in twenty years; they could be rotting from the inside out. Driftwood generally are lifeless in their work but haven't left their position. They have no direction and can't or won't move without a heavy current. Finally, ballast keeps the boat from shifting in high seas but more often just takes up space without helping make a difference. If there is too much ballast in the culture, it will sink.

The negative members of the network can have a devastating impact on the school. For example, in one school a teacher has the ability to sense the vulnerabilities of staff members and use those against them. This teacher attacks any new idea about instruction that could ameliorate problems. Faculty meetings are filled with silence, as staff have learned to avoid the well-aimed attacks.

In another example, a southern middle school is plagued with misinformation, as the informal network transmogrifies any message from administrators or optimistic teacher-leaders. The positive members of the staff are constantly having to correct negative reactions to inaccurate messages.

Without some positive members of the cultural network, new and old members of the culture can start to believe the negative fabrications and depictions of the school. This drags down the energy and motivation of even the strongest educator. Storytellers recount negative sagas and myths about the school. In these schools people view the world of their classrooms and students through negative or jaded filters. They perceive learning, motivation, or trust to be lost.

In one high school a distinctive story prevailed. It was constantly told and retold. It was the "Tale of the Thirty-Four Graduates of Westchester High School (a pseudonym) Who Were in Prison." This story shaped how people thought and felt about the students, their opportunities in life, and the potential of the school. To transform the culture a new view had to be developed. In another school, the major story about change focused on the innovative program that the principal brought in the 1970s that failed. This story of failure defined how staff thought about innovation and change for over two decades.

Heroes Are Antiheroic

Schools, like other social organizations, need heroes and heroines to define what is possible, to provide a standard to achieve. In one school, the main "hero" was a teacher who hadn't changed his instructional approach for twenty-three years. It was, to him, a badge of honor. He has actively resisted pressure from staff and administration alike to do something more educationally relevant and creative. In the school, he resisted change and championed stubbornness as a virtue, thus reinforcing similar negative stances in others. Without positive heroines the culture loses positive role models.

Few Positive Rituals, Traditions, or Ceremonies Exist

In many schools the year flows along as a demanding and difficult treadmill of drudgery and routine. No fun, no engaging traditions, no communal gatherings mark the movement of time or the recognition of accomplishments. Without traditional events full of fun and shared traditions, teachers, students, parents, and community residents remain isolated without collective ties. Without celebratory ceremonies to pep up spirit, honor the passage of time, or provide closure, schools become sterile, humdrum, joyless places.

In some schools, ceremonies even become negative countervalue events. Looking at the school's history only conjures up bitterness about "the good old days." In one school the end-of-the-year gathering was dropped. Once a vibrant time to celebrate 180 days of hard and productive work, the end-of-the-year barbecue failed to materialize because no one organized it. Even though the food had never been great—in fact, it was the subject of jokes—the talk and laughter had been infectious. Now the year ends are marked by teachers filling their wastebaskets with old reports; then they pack boxes with materials to take home. It is a sad and lonely ending.

In one high school, graduation itself became a negative experience. Students, and sometimes their parents, arrived drunk. Mice were let loose under the seats and belching became rampant. Graduation, which should be a time of joyful celebration, became a depressing series of pranks and malicious mischief.

Toxicity Transformed: Revisiting Jefferson High

In the late 1990s, the popular remedy for dealing with negative school environments was reconstitution—sort of a neutron bomb approach to school reform. Take out the people, leave the building intact, and start afresh with a new cast of characters. This may occasionally prove to be a viable solution. But cultural scripts and types are carried in people's heads, and cultural histories have a way of creeping back into a newly launched initiative. Remember that architecture, artifacts, alumni, and lingering cultural baggage can do a number on even the best-intended reconstitution effort.

Even though there is no tried-and-true formula for turning a negative situation around, school leaders might consider some lessons. Jefferson High, once a highly toxic place, offers a dramatic example of how a school can turn itself around. It's hard to imagine a worse situation.

Searching for something that might help the school improve, the principal and a steering group of teachers and staff called upon a nearby consultant. They asked him to visit the school, promising a preliminary meeting with no more than twenty teachers and staff. The consultant arrived to find himself face to face with all seventy faculty members who had been required to attend. As the consultant began to outline a possible change strategy, one older teacher, well known for his attacks on others, stood up and asked the consultant to leave. The consultant replied that he felt lucky to have that luxury. Everyone else in the room was stuck in a less desirable situation. Another teacher said, "Well you're being paid. At least stick around and earn your fee."

For the rest of the morning and afternoon the consultant held court, listened to concerns, and heard people blame everyone else for being the cause of the problem. The storyteller recounted all the negative events in detail. One older teacher, a school antiheroine, lent the consultant a card. It read, "There is no Santa Claus." At the end of the day, the steering committee agreed to take a second step. They decided to have a colleague of the consultant's interview every member of the faculty, staff, and administration, as well as the students, to gain a sense of the culture. Her one-on-one sessions made it possible for people to vent their frustrations, share their fears of the negativism continuing, and describe the few hopes and dreams a handful held onto.

After the interviews were examined, the consultants presented to the faculty the rather grim picture they had gathered. As they began to outline the litany of negative themes, the same angry teacher who disrupted the first session again attacked her. The other consultant intervened and waved his airline boarding pass for everyone to see: "I have a ticket out of here. None of you does." The group became silent.

After a few moments, the school's cultural priest stood up and said with uncharacteristic passion, "I'm not even sure I understand what these people are trying to do—but I'm all for it. You people have done nothing but complain, moan, and attack everything in sight for the past fifteen years." Other people offered their support. The meeting continued and people tried to see opportunities to overcome their hopelessness. After lunch, the group agreed on several concrete steps. First, four of the most negative faculty were asked by their colleagues not to join in meetings if they were going to continue to carp and complain. Then during the summer, teachers met and brainstormed strategies for the coming school year. Students were asked to join the meetings, many of which were held in teachers' homes.

In November of the next year, the consultants received an invitation to revisit the school. Upon their arrival it was hard to believe that this was the same place. Students were well behaved and excited about learning. The drop-out rate had been cut considerably. Daily attendance was at an all-time high. Teachers were more positive and enthusiastic about their teaching. The principal was actively involved in instructing and bringing parents into the school. Finally, in a reality check, the consultants sought out the former negaholic. Surprisingly, he was decidedly upbeat about the school's prognosis: "We were sinking. You tossed us some flotsam and jetsam. It's now our ship, and we're on our way. We pulled the stuff that was bobbing in the water together and built a raft."

After lunch that day, the faculty presented their first locally created inservice production, "Putting Magic Back Into the Classroom." The master of ceremonies was the school's priest, himself an accomplished magician. The sessions, many of them led by some of the schools previous "deadwood" were state of the art. The day ended with a party at an assistant principal's home. A veteran faculty member toasted the consultants: "We're not sure what happened here, but we sure like it. We have a whole new lease on life. We thank you for your involvement. We're not sure what you did. But we want you to know that the end result is ours. We did it on our own."

What happened at Jefferson is still something of a mystery. The key ingredients of the transformation were bringing toxicity to the surface, giving people a chance to vent, providing a chance to believe things could be better, and, finally, offering a more positive path and a large dose of hope. Sometimes, creating a crisis can provide the first step to cultural renewal. But in order to deal with toxicity, school leaders will have to risk the potential side effects of some very powerful interventions.

Antidotes for Negativism

To overcome cultural negativism is no easy task. It is often easier to continue to rely on the negative, pessimistic side of schools than to defend the positive or search for new possibilities. To transform negative cultures, school leaders must sometimes resort to extreme measures. They may need to take the following steps:

Confront the negativity head on; give people a chance to vent their venom in a public forum. Listen, challenge, and wait patiently for more positive sentiments to emerge.

Shield and support positive cultural elements and staff. In some schools those staff who believe in students, collaborate in the face of adversity, and fight for change are provided sanctuary, support, and encouragement.

Focus energy on the recruitment, selection, and retention of effective, positive staff. Replacing chronic negaholics who'll never embark on a more positive course may take time, but eventually the balance between hope and cynicism will change, giving rise to more interesting possibilities.

Rabidly celebrate the positive and the possible. Rebuild around new values and beliefs that are regularly and publicly recognized.

Consciously and directly focus on eradicating the negative and rebuilding around positive norms and beliefs. Ask staff to discuss what they want to bury—what negative, nasty values they want to give up.

Then, during retreats, faculty meetings, and informal discussions, keep the focus on the positive possibilities.

Develop new stories of success, renewal, and accomplishment. Find the small accomplishments and large initiatives that are beginning to emerge. Let everyone know what progress is being made. Eventually staff will start to believe in themselves and in the mission that brought them to education. Toxic cultures are destructive and demoralizing. Leaders, including administrators, teachers, and parents, can triumph over the negative if they are willing to join the fray with integrity.

Help those who might succeed and thrive in a new district make the move to a new school. If staff or administrators are more comfortable somewhere else, then they should be supported in finding a better place for themselves. Students and professional colleagues should not have to put up with the sustained negativity of poison people who may flourish in another environment. School leaders can help these people find other places to work.

———————

Transforming a toxic culture is a risky and scary undertaking. Many teachers and administrators have tried and failed; still others succeed without ever knowing why. It's not a job for the fainthearted or for those who need universal approval in the short term.

The process is akin to the metamorphosis of a butterfly. The caterpillar enters a cocoon. We call it the ritual process, in which an intense experience produces a dramatically different form—one that can soar to new places. The process occurs inside a school, sometimes assisted by outsiders, but is always led by those who have a vested interest in a new beginning. Like a butterfly, a school must be supported by its local environment in order to thrive. In the next chapter we see how schools connect with their community culture.

11

Connecting School and Community Culture

Like all organizations, schools have complex relationships with local "customers" and communities. The community provides many things the school needs and vice versa. The local community very often expects the school to provide a rational return in the form of student achievement. But there's more to it than that.

Communities often view schools as museums of virtue, storehouses of memories, and prime sources of local pride. People look to schools as a wellspring of hope. They look for assurance that local values are being transmitted and that the future will bear some connection with traditions of the past. Schools are highly symbolic institutions for any community, whether rural, suburban, or urban.

While policymakers clamor for change, parents and local residents are very often ambivalent about new approaches to teaching and testing. Paradoxically, they may want change as long as things don't look too different from what they know. They feel this paradox as a quest for innovative familiarity.

Schools also often want things from their parents and community. They want parents to help out in school, be involved in governance, encourage their children to try hard, or simply attend student performances in force. They want parents to provide coaching, encouragement, and inspiration to their children before they come to school. And they seek social and symbolic support for the hard work they do.

Good school leaders know the dance they must do. School leaders twirl to deliver reasonable achievement outcomes and then take a spinning pirouette to serve the deeper symbolic purpose of schools. Schools are simultaneously producers of learning and purveyors of meaning. Connections to the community seek both these ends.

School Culture as Local Theater

The culture of schools provides a sense of meaning internally as well as externally. A strong school identity helps students, teachers, staff, and leaders coalesce around a shared mission or purpose. But at the same time, strong school identity turned outward offers an opportunity to create faith and confidence among parents and local residents. The same cultural elements that anchor meaning inside a school—values, heroines, ritual, ceremony, and stories—can simultaneously convey a positive image externally. Here are some examples of what school leaders do:

School leaders market their schools. An elementary principal realized that her students, teachers, and staff—1,000 strong—constituted a powerful marketing department. Over dinner, at the local tavern, in the hair salon, or at the laundromat, school storytellers conveyed to others the daily or weekly happenings inside a school. The principal and other school leaders now keep staff, teachers, and students up to date on the memorable moments and anecdotes of success so they will have something positive to share.

School leaders build bonds with the community. In another elementary school, festivals are organized around the year's seasonal observances. Student performances of music, poetry, and art bring parents, citizens, and students together in a meaningful ceremony in which bonds are formed and shared values reinforced.

School leaders tie the history of the school to the history of the community. In a New York elementary school, parents, community residents, and students were brought together for a two-day exercise to reconstruct the school's history. They developed a chronology of school accomplishments and community growth on a single mural. That mural, depicting key events over time, now adorns the foyer.

School leaders connect to all members of the community. In a California high school, the principal accidentally stumbled on what the school might do to strengthen its relationships with a large, and heretofore largely antagonistic, nearby retirement community. As he walked to the parking lot at the end of the day, two senior citizens approached him and thanked him profusely for "such a wonderful gesture." Although he had no idea what they were talking about, he acknowledged their gratitude. As he walked to his car, he suddenly realized what they were talking about. As a reward to the high school senior class, parking spaces had been labeled "Private Parking—Seniors Only." He later met with the director of activities and established a "surrogate grandparent program."

Faith Popcorn's prediction is that in the next decade consumers' or clients' confidence and loyalty will be given to organizations with a "soul." Her advice: "If you don't have one, you better get one quickly" (1991, p. 162).

For many schools, this will require soul-searching to refine or revitalize deep cultural values and purposes. At the journey's zenith, internal meaning, cohesion, and commitment will be apparent. Equally important, a bedrock identity becomes a solid foundation for projecting a positive image. In communities where a school's meaningful virtues are widely broadcast to external constituencies, a robust sense of connection will reduce overdependence on test scores and other measures to determine a school's real worth. Balancing "seeing is believing" with "believing is seeing" will help encourage a stronger connection between school and community culture.

Bridging the Parent-School Gap

Across nearly all studies of school effectiveness a key factor stands out: school performance and parent involvement are intimately intertwined (Levine and Lezotte, 1990). Having parents involved in schools can narrow cultural gaps that arise when parents are held at arm's length or feel apathetic toward a school or their children's learning. Only when a solid and positive partnership prevails between schools and parents will education flourish. The community exchanges many things with the school.

Schools need strong, organic linkages between schools and parents. They need parents who see the importance of schools and impart this to their children. On the other side, parents need schools who understand their perspectives and help them with their children.

In her study of parent-school relationships in northern California's inner-city schools, Claire Smrekar found a troubling pattern in some schools. Often, administrators and teachers held error-ridden stereotypes of parents—stereotypes that broke the bond between school and parents. The educators' assumptions were that parents don't become involved because they are either apathetic about their children's education, too lazy to get involved, or both. Parents didn't see it the same way. Compare those observations with some of the comments of parents in her study.

Parents valued education. They reported: "Well, nowadays you have to have a good education to do anything in life. You even have to have a degree to dig ditches. Back then, you didn't really have to have a good education, just a good backbone to do anything. School is important because you gotta live, and to live you gotta work, unless you get into that selling dope like those other (people) that line the streets" (Smrekar, 1991, p. 14).

Parents wanted to help their children with school. They said: "My job is sending my kids to school. I can't help them with their homework because I have had little schooling myself. I ask my children how they are doing, what homework they have, and have they done it. My job is to find out if they have any notes from school, and to keep on top of what is happening there" (p. 20).

Parents wanted to assist in schools. They stated: "Mostly parent involvement is giving money because if you go up there and say a lot of things, then the teachers feel like you're trying to take over their jobs" (p. 26).

Parents wanted to feel comfortable at school activities. They said: "Okay, when you go to school for a school meeting, you feel like, it's uncomfortable. When you're in a room with everybody around you, or sitting in a straight row—you're uncomfortable, and you can't really say what you want to say. You feel tense, like the army or something. Make us feel like we're a part of something" (p. 27).

Rather than being the disinterested, apathetic people that school leaders sometimes imagine, parents are vitally interested in their children's education. They are unsure of what they are supposed to do, but pretty sure that they're not always wanted, welcomed, or listened to.

Contrast this pattern to Carlton School, a northern California magnet school serving a mixed-ethnic population with a large number of single-parent families (Smrekar, 1996). At Carlton, parents are deeply involved in the school, and the school is deeply involved with parents.

Parents sign a contract with teachers and students specifying respective responsibilities and mutual expectations.

A telephone chain alerts parents of school events. Notes sent home must be returned with a parent signature the next day. Otherwise, the students have several minutes subtracted from recess.

Weekly reports go home with each student, detailing the week's performance.

Parents are encouraged to visit the school any time. They are comfortable stopping in whenever their schedule permits.

Parent or student conferences last at least thirty minutes.

Parents must give forty hours a year to attend school events: fundraisers, meetings, and social get-togethers. But they gladly do it.

A mutually created, shared social tapestry bonds Carlton parents, teachers, and students together. There are shared expectations, meaningful interactions, rituals of involvement, and celebrations of accomplishment. Educators and community relationships thrive in a jointly controlled, emotionally satisfying, spiritually uplifting educational community. As they describe it: "The teachers and the children and the parents. It belongs to us. It's ours. You ask the teachers around here. This is like family to us" (Smrekar, 1996, p. 11).

Many schools put in place some of the same kinds of efforts to involve parents: parent handbooks, back-to-school nights, lunches, principal chats, assemblies, newsletters, school advisory committees, fundraisers, parent centers. But too often these are the more mechanical, go-through-the-motions initiatives. They are devoid of shared meaning and the more organic, communal values that truly bring people together for a shared purpose. An overly mechanical approach is incapable of drawing parents into an organic relationship with the school. Part of the school culture must reach out and connect with parents.

Particularly when the school community consists of diverse cultures, something special must be done to lay the groundwork for a common mission and to build an inclusive, cohesive community. These outreach efforts need not be extravagant. Simple things can go a long way. Two examples follow.

A New York public school experienced a major shift in the ethnic makeup of the surrounding community. Once primarily African American, the community now consisted of a large number of Korean Americans. Despite many attempts to draw the parents into the school, nothing seemed to work. At a faculty meeting, a teacher suggested that maybe the faculty and staff should learn to speak some

Korean. The principal offered to have Berlitz come to the school to provide language instruction. Someone else suggested that they pay students after school to do the job. Everyone agreed. Shortly after the classes began, parents started to visit the school.

In another school, leaders converted an old classroom into a parent center. Freshly painted walls, nice furniture (donated by local businesses and families), books, videotapes on parenting, coffee, and refreshments provided a place for parents to visit with teachers, read to their kids, or talk with other parents. It became a well-visited social center creating a solid and cohesive parent network.

School Culture, Internal and External

It is easy for cohesive school cultures to become exclusionary, distant, walled off from the community. In some schools the culture encourages staff to draw together and shut out parents. Different languages, interaction styles, and educational beliefs too often create a sharp divide between professionals working inside schools and parents waiting outside. Building a cohesive school community means shaping a culture that reaches out and touches everyone: students, teachers, staff, administrators, parents, and community.

Symbolic bonds need to connect across the school's perimeter. They need to incorporate all constituents in a shared effort to both achieve results and to create an institution that produces widespread faith, hope, and confidence. Doing both requires the active involvement of everyone. The same sensitivity required for shaping culture internally must be applied to linking the school to parents and other members of the community.

12

Conclusion
The Future of Schools

There is nothing like a young life with great potential. And a sound education is one of the best ways to ensure that every promising young person comes to fruition as a well-adjusted, fully skilled adult.

Students deserve the best schools we can give them—schools full of heart, soul, and ample opportunities to learn and grow. Too often, students are being shortchanged. They are stifled by sterile, toxic places that turn them against learning rather than turn them on to it.

Our efforts at educational improvement often do not work to guarantee good schools for everyone. Reforms that focus only on changing structures or school governance will never succeed in building positive organic forms that will serve all our students. Reforms that bring new technologies or higher standards won't succeed without being embedded in supportive, spirit-filled cultures. Schools won't become what students deserve until cultural patterns and ways are shaped to support learning. Leadership from throughout the school will be needed to build and maintain such positive, purposeful places to learn and grow.

As we face the new millennium, school leaders will grapple with both paradox and opportunity. How well they balance opposing forces and find promising pathways will have a tremendous impact on America's future.

Paradox, Culture, and Leadership

In the future, school leaders will face five central paradoxes in their work. As leaders, they cannot solve a paradox the way a problem is solved. A leader must discover ways to harmonize and find the right balance among conflicting values. The five paradoxes are as follows:

Paradox of purpose. Leaders need to build and maintain a shared purpose while encouraging enough creative diversity to ensure continued growth for students and staff. Shared purpose is key to quality schools, but it is equally important to nurture diverse views, be open to innovation, and encourage flexibility for the sake of progress.

Paradox of people. Leaders must be caring and supportive of people who work in schools but also must champion and protect the integrity and common good of the institution. This is one of leadership's deepest and most challenging paradoxes. As schools empower, motivate, and nurture staff and parents, it must be for the common good of students, the school, and society at large.

Paradox of change. Leaders must perpetuate what is thriving in the present while reaching for what may be even better in the future. They must both embrace change and remain the same. They must balance the status quo with future improvements.

Paradox of action. Leaders must take time to reflect on purpose and potential but must also make decisions and take action. It is always a balancing act: reflecting ideas about what to do and implementing what appears to be a satisfactory decision (Palmer, 1990). Leaders must do both well. They must visualize new purposes and better directions while bringing new possibilities to reality.

Paradox of leading. Leadership must come from the principal, but he or she cannot be the only source of leadership. To sustain strong, positive cultures, leadership must come from everyone.

New Opportunities, New Challenges

In the new millennium, school leaders will also encounter a number of critical opportunities to lead their schools. If not addressed, the opportunities, which are described next, will be lost.

Opportunity of purpose. Central to successful schools is a powerful sense of purpose that is focused on students and on learning. Developing and articulating a deep sense of purpose is the foundation of a strong culture.

Opportunity of place. Schools are complex, demanding institutions. School leaders must make these special places where students, staff, parents, and community members feel welcome, safe, and appreciated. A positive "ethos of place" should permeate everything that goes on.

Opportunity of people. People are the central resources in any organization. When leaders invest in a culture that nurtures and challenges staff, students, and community, it pays off in learning outcomes. Putting time into building a culture that motivates and inspires people is the venture capital of schools.

Opportunity of competence. Human beings crave competence. Everyone wants to do well. The challenge and opportunity for school leaders is to nourish the competence of staff and students in their work, their thinking, and their daily actions. Through competence comes achievement.

Opportunity of commitment. School leaders will need to build or, in some cases, resurrect commitment to schools and to education. The past decade has disheartened some about the possibilities of education and the potential of schools. School leaders from every corner of the school need to relentlessly build commitment.

Opportunity of celebration. School leaders need to find exciting ways to celebrate accomplishments of the culture. Schools are living, breathing organisms. In order to thrive, people need to come together in community to celebrate accomplishment, hard work, and dedication. By celebrating the best of what the school has done in ceremony, song, or words, everyone exalts in the accomplishments of compatriots.

Opportunity of caring. Finally, school leaders face the need to bring caring back to schools (Noddings, 1992; Beck, 1994). Schools and classrooms demand much from their inhabitants. It is hard work to teach and to learn. By establishing schools as caring places, the culture can only become more humane and kind.

Paradox versus opportunity, standards versus spirit, test scores versus stories—the list of dilemmas school leaders will face in the coming century goes on and on. But in our view, unless we can restore the sacred stature of education, very little will help us achieve our hopes and dreams. Teachers need once again to believe in themselves and relish the opportunities they have to make a real difference. Communities need to reexamine the role schools play in society, that is, the role of balancing cognitive achievement with character development.

We began this book by taking another look at what really makes businesses succeed. Too often, schools are asked to master the wrong lessons about what makes a successful organization tick. Clear goals, rational structures, high standards, and accountability are only part of why a business succeeds. The real lesson is how business leaders are able to infuse passion and purpose into an enterprise and to build a common spirit and cohesive culture.

Herb Kelleher, CEO of Southwest Airlines, gave a speech to employees on the occasion of the launch of Southwest's "Symbol of Freedom" campaign. He reminded people of Southwest's central mission: making it possible for anyone to visit a relative, attend a wedding, be at a friend's funeral, or go somewhere just for the fun of it. "Giving people the freedom to fly is," he said, "Southwest's higher calling and ennobling purpose" (Kelleher, 1997). As Southwest's employees come to work each day, they are not just answering phones, taking tickets, loading bags, or fueling aircraft. Their collective efforts are making it possible for others to enjoy the fruits of life.

In education, our higher calling or ennobling purpose is even more majestic. We are giving young people a chance to thrive and succeed in the world. Tracy Kidder, in his book *Among School Children* (1989), paints education's sacred mission in lyric prose:

> Teachers [and other school leaders] usually have no way of knowing that they have made a difference in a child's life, even when they have made a dramatic one. But for children who are used to thinking of themselves as stupid or not worth talking to or deserving rape and beatings, a good teacher can provide an astonishing revelation. A good teacher can give a child at least a chance to feel "*She* thinks I'm worth something, maybe I am." Good teachers [and good school leaders] put snags in the river of children passing by, and over the years, they redirect hundreds of lives. Many people find it easy to imagine unseen webs of malevolent conspiracy in the world, and they are not always wrong. But there is also an innocence that conspires to hold humanity together, and it is made up of people who can never fully know the good they have done. [pp. 312–313]

The core leadership challenge of the coming millennium is to build schools in which every child can grow and every teacher can make a difference. Such sentiments flourish in a culture where learning and caring are valued and where stories, rituals, and ceremonies provide zest and buoyancy to the world's most sacred profession. School leaders can make a difference by restoring hope, faith, and a shared spirit to the place called school.

Strong cultures produce dense leadership—every member becomes champion, visionary, and poet. As teachers and parents become leaders—cultural icons for the deeper values of the school—the school becomes more than a building with instructional materials. It becomes an institution with history, values, purpose, and pride.

Conclusion

As we have seen in the preceding chapters, school cultures are complex systems. Leaders need the skills and knowledge to uncover a culture's deeper history. They need the techniques to assess current conditions and values. And most important, they require the ability to be symbolic leaders and cultural reinforcers in their daily work. For some, these skills can be developed on the job; others will go through preparation programs. But many will need in-depth professional development opportunities with adequate time to reflect, analyze, and interpret their culture.

If a company can motivate employees to pour their hearts into selling coffee (or motorcycles or cars), then schools should be able to motivate staff to pour themselves into teaching. Schools that are toxic should be provided the support, leadership, and charge to renew themselves. Schools that are dangerous to the health and learning of students and staff alike need to be transformed or reformed into positive, meaningful institutions. All our children deserve the best schools we can provide.

References

Barth, R. S. *Improving Schools from Within*. San Francisco: Jossey-Bass, 1991.

Beck, L. G. *Reclaiming Educational Administration as a Caring Profession*. New York: Teachers College Press, 1994.

Bissinger, H. G. *Friday Night Lights: A Town, a Team, and a Dream*. New York: HarperPerrenial, 1991.

Bolman, L., and Deal, T. E. *Reframing Organizations: Artistry, Choice, and Leadership*. (2nd ed.) San Francisco: Jossey-Bass, 1997.

Boloz, S. "The C Diet." Unpublished manuscript, 1997.

Bower, M. *Will to Manage*. New York: McGraw-Hill, 1996.

Boyd-Dimock, V., and Hord, S. "Schools as Learning Communities." Issues . . . About Change. [www.sedl.org./changes/issues/issues 47.html], 1994–1995.

Bryk, A., Lee, V. E., and Holland, P. B. *Catholic Schools and the Common Good*. Cambridge, Mass.: Harvard University Press, 1993.

Carter-Scott, C. *The Corporate Negaholic*. New York: Villard Books, 1991.

Clark, B. "The Organizational Saga in Higher Education." *Administrative Science Quarterly*, 1972, *17*, 178–184.

Collins, J. C., and Porras, J. I. *Build to Last: Successful Habits of Visionary Companies*. New York: Harper Business, 1997.

Cutler, W. W., III. "Cathedral of Culture: The Schoolhouse in American Educational Thought and Practice Since 1820." *History of Education Quarterly*, 1989, *29*, 1–40

Deal, T. E., and Kennedy, A. A. *Corporate Cultures: The Rites and Rituals of Corporate Life*. Reading, Mass.: Addison-Wesley, 1982.

Deal, T. E., and Key, M. K. *Corporate Celebration: Play, Purpose, and Profit at Work*. San Francisco: Berrett-Koehler, 1998.

Deal, T. E., and Peterson, K. D. *The Principal's Role in Shaping School Culture*. Washington, D.C.: Office of Educational Research and Improvement, U.S. Department of Education, 1990.

Deal, T. E., and Peterson, K. D. *The Leadership Paradox: Balancing Logic and Artistry in Schools*. San Francisco: Jossey-Bass, 1994.

Deal, T. E., and Peterson, K. D. "Principals: Leaders of Change." *The Video Journal of Education*, 1996, 5(7).

Driver, C. E., and Levin, H. M. "The Dilemma of Principal Succession in Restructuring Schools." Unpublished manuscript, Accelerated Schools Project, Stanford University, 1997.

Firestone, W. A., and Wilson, B. L. "Using Bureaucratic and Cultural Linkages to Improve Instruction: The Principal's Contribution." *Educational Administration Quarterly*, 1985, 21(2), 7–30.

Fullan, M. "Leadership for the 21st Century: Breaking the Bonds of Dependency." *Educational Leadership*, April 1998, pp. 6–10.

Geertz, C. M. *The Interpretation of Cultures*. New York: Basic Books, 1973.

Hopfenberg, W. S., Levin, H. M., and Associates. *The Accelerated Schools Resource Guide*. San Francisco: Jossey-Bass, 1993.

Johnson, M. "Hollibrook Elementary School: A Case Study." In R. T. Clift and P. W. Thurston (eds.), *Distributed Leadership: School Improvement Through Collaboration*. Greenwich, Conn.: JAI Press, 1995.

Johnson, S. M. *Teachers at Work: Achieving Success in Our Schools*. New York: Basic Books, 1990.

Kaufman, B. *Up the Down Staircase*. New York: Avon, 1966.

Kelleher, H. "Southwest: A Symbol of Freedom." Internal publication of Southwest Airlines, 1997. Video.

Kidder, T. *Among Schoolchildren*. Boston: Houghton Mifflin, 1989.

Kilmann, R. H. "Five Steps for Closing Culture-Gaps." In R. H. Kilmann., M. J. Saxton, and R. Serpa and Associates (eds.). *Gaining Control of the Corporate Culture*. San Francisco: Jossey-Bass, 1985.

Kotter, J. P., and Heskett, J. L. *Corporate Culture and Performance*. New York: Free Press, 1992.

Kübler-Ross, E. *On Death and Dying*. New York: Macmillan, 1969.

Leithwood, K., and Jantzi, D. "Transformational Leadership: How Principals Can Help Reform School Cultures." *School Effectiveness and School Improvement*, 1990, 1, 249–280.

Levine, D. U., and Lezotte, L. W. *Unusually Effective Schools: A Review and Analysis of Research and Practice*. Madison, Wis.: National Center for Effective Schools Research and Development, 1990.

Little, J. W. "Norms of Collegiality and Experimentation: Workplace Conditions of School Success. *American Educational Research Journal*, 1982, *19*(3), 325–340.

Lortie, D. C. *Schoolteacher*. Chicago: University of Chicago Press, 1975.

Louis, K. S., and Miles, M. B. *Improving the Urban High School: What Works and Why*. New York: Teachers College Press, 1990.

Martinez, L. Unpublished doctoral dissertation, Peabody College, Vanderbilt University, Nashville, Tenn., 1989.

McLaughlin, M. W. "What Matters Most in Teachers' Workplace Conditions?" In J. W. Little and M. W. McLaughlin (eds.), *Teachers' Work: Individuals, Colleagues, and Contents*. New York: Teachers College Press, 1993.

McLaughlin, M. Keynote address at the annual conference of the National Staff Development Council, Chicago, Dec. 1995.

Meier, D. *The Power of Their Ideas: Lessons for America from a Small School in Harlem*. Boston: Beacon Press, 1995.

Meier, D., and Schwartz, P. "Central Park East Secondary School: The Hard Part Is Making It Happen in Democratic Schools." In M. W. Apple and J. A. Beane (eds.), *Democratic Schools*. Alexandria, Va.: Association for Supervision and Curriculum Development, 1995.

Newmann, F. M., and Associates. *Authentic Instruction: Restructuring Schools for Intellectual Quality*. San Francisco: Jossey-Bass, 1996.

Noddings, N. *The Challenge to Care in Schools: An Alternative Approach to Education*. New York: Teachers College Press, 1992.

Ott, J. S. *The Organizational Culture Perspective*. Pacific Grove, Calif.: Brooks/Cole, 1989.

Palmer, P. J. *The Active Life: Wisdom for Work, Creativity, and Caring*. New York: HarperCollins, 1990.

Peterson, K. D., and Bamburg, J. "Case Studies in Successful Urban School Leadership." Unpublished manuscript, North Central Regional Educational Laboratory, Oak Brook, Ill., 1993.

Peterson, K. D., and Brietzke, R. *Building Collaborative Cultures: Seeking Ways to Reshape Urban Schools*. Urban Monograph Series. Oak Brook, Ill.: North Central Regional Educational Laboratory, 1994.

Pondy, L. R. "Leadership as a Language Game." In M. McCall and M. Lambert (eds.), *Leadership: Where Else Can We Go?* Durham, N.C.: Duke University Press, 1976.

Popcorn, F. *The Popcorn Report*. New York: Doubleday, 1991.

Purkey, S. C., and Smith, M. S. "Effective Schools: A Review." *Elementary School Journal*, 1983, *83*(4), 427–452.

Reitzug, R. C., and Reeves, J. E. "'Miss Lincoln Doesn't Teach Here': A Descriptive Narrative and Conceptual Analysis of a Principal's Symbolic Leadership Behavior." *Educational Administration Quarterly*, 1992, 28(2), 185–219.

Ricks, T. E. *Making the Corps*. New York: Scribner, 1997.

Rossman, G. B., Corbett, H. D., and Firestone, W. A. *Change and Effectiveness in Schools*. Albany: State University of New York Press, 1988.

Rutter, M., Maughan, B., Mortimore, P., Ouston, J., and Smith, A. *Fifteen Thousand Hours*. Cambridge, Mass.: Harvard University Press, 1979.

Saphier, J., and King, M. "Good Seeds Grow in Strong Cultures." *Educational Leadership*, March 1985, pp. 72–75.

Sashkin, M., and Walberg, H. *Educational Leadership and School Culture*. Berkeley, Calif.: McCutchan, 1993.

Schein, E. H. *Organizational Culture and Leadership*. San Francisco: Jossey-Bass, 1985.

Schein, E. H. *Organizational Culture and Leadership*. (2nd ed.) San Francisco: Jossey-Bass, 1992.

Schultz, H., and Yang, D. J. *Pour Your Heart into It: How Starbucks Built a Company One Cup at a Time*. New York: Hyperion, 1997.

Smrekar, C. "The Voices of Parents: Rethinking the Intersection of Family and School." Unpublished manuscript, 1991.

Smrekar, C. *The Impact of School Choice and Community: In the Interest of Families and Schools*. Albany: State University of New York Press, 1996.

Trice, H. M., and Beyer, J. M. "Using Six Organizational Rites to Change Culture." In R. H. Kilmann, M. J. Saxton, R. Serpa, and Associates (eds.), *Gaining Control of the Corporate Culture*. San Francisco: Jossey-Bass, 1985.

Vydra, J. "Three Cases of Culture Building." Unpublished manuscript, 1998.

Waller, W. *The Sociology of Teaching*. New York: Wiley, 1932.

Index